21 Days to *Better* Fitness

Books in the 21-Day Series

Proven Plan or Beginning New Habits

21 Days to *Better* Fitness

Maggie Greenwood-Robinson

Series Editor
Dan Benson

ZondervanPublishingHouse
Grand Rapids, Michigan

A Division of HarperCollinsPublishers

21 Days to Better Fitness
Copyright © 1998 by Maggie Greenwood-Robinson

Requests for information should be addressed to:

 ZondervanPublishingHouse
Grand Rapids, Michigan 49530

ISBN: 0-310-21750-4

Published in association with the literary agency of Alive Communications, Inc., 1465 Kelly Johnson Blvd. #320, Colorado Springs, CO 80920

Interior design by Sherri L. Hoffman

Printed in the United States of America

To my husband, Jeffry,
my father, Thomas Edward Greenwood, and
in loving memory of my mother,
Margaret Ten Hagen Greenwood

CONTENTS

ACKNOWLEDGMENTS

*"Return, faithless people," declares the L*ORD*, "for I am your husband. I will choose you—one from a town and two from a clan—and bring you to Zion. Then I will give you shepherds after my own heart, who will lead you with knowledge and understanding" (Jer. 3:14–15).*

When I returned to God, he fulfilled in my life the promise of Jeremiah 3:14–15. He put three shepherds in my life who have guided me with knowledge and understanding, and to them goes my deepest appreciation:

Dr. Stephen Schwambach, senior pastor of Bethel Temple in Evansville, Indiana, from whom I first heard God's life-changing, life-saving Gospel that lead me to commit my life to Christ. Steve and his wife, Judy, are a constant source of inspiration to me and my husband.

Teresa Patchin, minister of music at Bethel Temple, who shepherded me into a small group (an answer to prayer) and helped me grow deeper in the Christian faith.

Bret Nicholson, college and career pastor at Bethel Temple, who was becoming a shepherd as I was becoming a sheep. I am indebted to Bret and his wife, Krista, for their abiding friendship and unswerving dedication to teaching God's truth.

I also owe a debt of gratitude to Kathy Yanni, Alive Communications, for believing in me; to Dan Benson, the 21-Day series editor, for his uplifting encouragement; and to the staff at Zondervan Publishing House, the most author-focused group with whom I have ever worked.

Above all, I thank my ultimate Shepherd, Jesus Christ, for the opportunity to share what the Bible says about living a more beneficial lifestyle, and I give him the credit for this book and any lives that it may touch.

PREFACE

The Word on Fitness

The Best-Kept Motivational Secret
Everyone Should Know

How often have you said to yourself, "Today, I will start eating right" or "Today, I will start exercising regularly"? But then the days pass without so much as a salad or a sit-up. Getting fit takes too much work and takes much too long. Or does it?

Motivational experts tell us that it takes just twenty-one days to form new habits. So if you can eat right and exercise regularly, day by day, for three weeks, you can turn good intentions into second-nature habits.

21 Days to Better Fitness teaches you exactly how to do that. It's a simple approach that makes habit-change possible (and easy). You'll break free from habits that you may have found impossible to change in the past. By the end of 21 days, you'll be amazed at the differences in your appearance, energy levels, and overall health. You'll experience a fitness you can see and feel.

SO HOW DO YOU START?

By taking it easy. That's right. No abrupt or sudden changes in lifestyle or behavior. No grandiose pledges to lose 20 pounds in a month ... exercise super-hard every day for two hours ... or never eat cheesecake again. For example: Instead of saying, "I'm giving up junk food forever," tell yourself, "Today, I will make healthier food choices. If that works, I will do the same tomorrow." You'll ease into new eating and exercise habits with small, conservative steps. Small changes, successfully completed, build confidence.

Some experts advise tackling only one bad habit at a time. Yet research studies say the opposite: Working on more than one pays big dividends. That's because bad health habits tend to stick together and negatively reinforce each other. Overeating and underexercising, for example, seem to go hand in hand. So, by exercising, you'll naturally want to start eating better. Voilà: two bad habits licked at once.

YOU'RE NOT POWERLESS OVER YOUR HEALTH

One of the chief reasons we may not be as healthy as we could be is because of the lifestyle choices we make and the bad habits we develop as a result of those choices. In a fitness career that has included writing ten books and many articles on diet, exercise, and nutrition, I grew fascinated by the connection between lifestyle and health and went on to write my doctoral dissertation on nutrition in the management and prevention of chronic diseases. It became very clear to me that by making healthy choices, consistently, people have a huge say in their present and future health. But I'm not coming at this from a purely professional or academic point of view. I've been where many of you are today: I'm a former couch potato, binge eater, eating-disorder patient, and a chronic on-again, off-again dieter. Believe me, I understand the uphill battles and the day-to-day struggles with diet and exercise issues. If I was able to change, so can you. And it's not too late.

In this book, you'll learn how to change your bad eating and exercise habits—two of the most health-destructive behaviors around. Consider this: Four of the ten leading causes of death in the United States—heart disease, stroke, cancer, and diabetes—are all linked to bad eating habits. Poor nutrition is also implicated in obesity, a disease that in sheer numbers and its toll in death and disability has reached crisis proportions in the United States.

Medical experts now estimate that 58 million adults—more than a third of our population—are overweight or obese. Beyond being a mere problem of appearance, obesity is a serious health risk for Americans of all ages—a risk that's linked to heart disease, high blood pressure, stroke, diabetes, gallbladder disease, mental health problems, and many cancers. After smoking, which causes an estimated 500,000 deaths annually, weight-related illnesses are the second-leading cause of death in the United States, costing 300,000 lives each year.

There's more: A recent report issued by the U.S. Surgeon General says that more than 60 percent of American adults are not getting enough exercise every day to stay healthy, and 25 percent do not exercise at all. This first-ever report noted that Americans are becoming a nation of couch potatoes, at risk for an increasing number of life-shortening illnesses. Perhaps more shocking, an estimated 250,000 deaths in the U.S. each year can be linked to a lack of exercise, according to the Centers for Disease Control and Prevention.

We're killing ourselves with our own bad habits.

Discouraging as this sounds on the surface, it reveals some positive news: You can fend off disease and stretch out your productive, healthy years by eliminating your careless habits and changing your lifestyle. And you can do it in just 21 days.

STAYING POWER

Now ... where do you get the staying power to stick to the 21-day plan? Your motivation might come from without—external situations that spur you to action, such as doctor's orders or pressure to please your spouse. Or your motivation might come from within: You decide to eat right and exercise because you want to do something positive for yourself.

Both types of motivators are effective; they prompt you to take action—at least, initially. But they often involve that kind of grit-your-teeth-and-do-it effort that ultimately fails to produce any lasting results.

What you need is staying power from above.

Getting fit doesn't come naturally—you probably know that from previous attempts to get in shape—it comes *supernaturally*. God provides the staying power you need to pursue a healthier lifestyle. Ask him to give you the strength you need to break your destructive health habits.

That may sound like a radical motivational concept to you until you realize something vital to your success: God doesn't intend for you or me to live with little regard for our own health and fitness. He cares about every choice we make—including health choices—and gives us principles in his Word to help us make choices that are in our best interest. If you live your life according to God's principles for physical and spiritual health, you can achieve better fitness, starting now.

A great way to begin this book is by focusing on several key principles from God's Word. They'll help you see that God wants you to take care of your body—and why.

Principle 1: Value the Body God Has Given You

A fashionable saying these days is: "It's my body, and I'll do whatever I want with it." And so people overeat, don't exercise, abuse alcohol, smoke, take dangerous drugs, have abortions, engage in promiscuous sex, and so forth.

But Paul teaches us: "Do you not know that your body is a temple of the Holy Spirit, who is in you, whom you have received from God? You are not your own; you were bought at a price. Therefore honor God with your body" (1 Cor. 6:19–20). God created you. He owns your body and sent his Holy Spirit to live inside you, to comfort you, counsel you, and guide you.

Many times we violate our bodies by pursuing health-destructive behaviors. In essence, we are defiling the home God has made within us. Rather than hurt your body through reckless disregard, honor God by taking care of his dwelling place with positive health behaviors.

Principle 2: Your Body Is an Instrument of Ministry

The accounts of Jesus' miraculous healings in the New Testament are a rich source of instruction on physical and spiritual health. Luke, a physician, describes the following medical miracle: "Simon's mother-in-law was suffering from a high fever, and they asked Jesus to help her. So he bent over her and rebuked the fever, and it left her. She got up at once and began to wait on them" (Luke 4:38–39).

The healing of Simon's mother-in-law is miraculous. But notice what happens after the fever leaves her: She gets up immediately and starts to serve her guests. She didn't loll around in bed; she didn't have to. Jesus restored her health so instantaneously and completely that she was strong enough to get up and serve God and her family—right away.

God expects you to serve, yet you can't do it very well if you're bedridden, fatigued, or sick all the time. When you're healthy and strong, you can better fulfill your ministry of service to him, whether that involves volunteering in the church nursery, teaching a Sunday school class, working in the mission field, or serving in the most important place of all: your home.

Principle 3: Make the Best Health Choices You Can Each Day

Can't you picture it? God planted a lush garden in Eden, dotted with trees full of mouth-watering fruit—a real smorgasbord. Then God gave Adam and Eve permission to eat from any tree, except one. But Adam and Eve couldn't see the forest for that one tree. You know the rest of the story and its consequences for humanity.

From a health perspective, we're in a kind of Garden of Eden. We can eat greasy, artery-clogging foods every night, or fill up on health-giving fresh fruits and vegetables. We can collapse on the couch after work, or go walk or jog a couple of miles. It's our choice, and we can suffer or savor the consequences.

God has given us free will—the power to choose. But we get into trouble when our choices conflict with God's. Our choices can make us sick and unhealthy. Part of God's will for our lives is that we make positive choices that promote better health. As we put our lives in God's hands, our self-destructive habits gradually lose their grip on us, and we can begin to lead healthier, more peaceful lives.

Principle 4: Trust God With Every Aspect of Your Life

When Paul told the Thessalonians, "May your whole spirit, soul and body be kept blameless at the coming of our Lord Jesus Christ" (1 Thess. 5:23), he reminded us that God must be involved in every dimension of our lives—spiritual, emotional, and physical.

Sometimes we think God is not concerned with our physical health, only our spiritual. But notice what the disciple John writes to Gaius: "Dear friend, I pray that you may enjoy good health and that all may go well with you, even as your soul is getting along well" (3 John 2).

These verses speak volumes about God's attitude toward health. He cares about your spiritual and physical well-being. At the core of Christianity is the story of God coming to earth in the flesh and walking among us, fully man yet fully God— fully physical and fully spiritual. During his ministry on earth, Jesus preached and healed. He came to save our souls—and our bodies. God takes the physical part of our existence very seriously. So should we.

This is not to say that if we always make the right health choices, we'll always be disease free. Poor lifestyle choices are a major source of illness. And it's true that if you practice good health habits, you're more likely to stay well. But there's no guarantee. There are other reasons for sickness that we cannot fully comprehend on this side of heaven—and they may be among the "secret things" that belong to the Lord spoken of in Deuteronomy 29:29. That's why we must trust God absolutely in whatever happens, for he is working his divine purpose.

Principle 5: Transformation Begins When You Recognize the Need for Change and Ask God for Help

Bad health habits and the sickness they cause can only begin to be changed when we admit their presence and ask for God's help. A beautiful example is the story in Mark 10:46–52 of Bartimaeus, a blind beggar sitting by the road. As Jesus approached, accompanied by a crowd, Bartimaeus cried out, "Son of David, have mercy on me!" He asked Jesus to restore his sight—a specific prayer for a specific problem. As a result of his faith, Jesus restored his sight. So full of gratitude was Bartimaeus that he began to follow Jesus.

At the beginning of the story, Bartimaeus is "by the road"—in a position to be helped but going nowhere; by the end, he is "on the road" to a fresh start in life. To get on the right road, we must come to Jesus in faith and ask for his help with our specific problem. God can't change us unless we're ready for him to do so. As the story of Bartimaeus shows, change comes from God. Only when we get on his path does the process of restoration truly begin. It continues when we follow Jesus, walking in faith with him daily and asking for his guidance every step along the way.

If you're ready to get on the right road and change your poor health habits, you might want to begin with the following prayer:

> Lord Jesus,
>
> Forgive me for living apart from your will. Starting now, I want to live as you intend for me to live, free of self-

destructive habits and behaviors. I put my life into your hands, knowing that through your power all things are possible. Strengthen me in all the weak moments. Direct my steps. Change me into the kind of person you desire me to be, that I may know and do your will and bring honor to you. These things I ask in your precious name and according to your divine will. Amen.

A STEP-BY-STEP, DAY-BY-DAY APPROACH

The 21-day program is a workable, progressive approach that's very easy to follow, with practical suggestions to guide you along the way. Each day, the program builds on the prior day, reinforcing the good habits you've put into practice and giving you confidence to continue.

Once you start following the 21-day plan, you'll begin to feel better just a few days into the first week. Best of all, it helps you improve your health and fitness in the light of Scripture. Follow this plan, and you'll live a healthier, happier life, beginning now.

DAY 1

Nothing-to-It Nutrition

High-Octane Foods That Build Health

Eat this. Don't eat that. Nutritional advice is confusing and contradictory. What's a body to do? I will decode nutrition for you by reducing it to two simple guidelines:

1. Go For the Pure, Not for the Processed

Starting today, eat foods as close as possible to the way God created them. Some examples: raw fruits; natural juices; fresh, frozen, and lightly cooked vegetables; natural, unrefined whole grains; unoiled, unsalted nuts and seeds. Why is this a big deal? Because your body uses pure, natural food much more efficiently than it uses processed, chemical-laden food, such as refined cereals, commercially baked goods, or fat-, sugar-, and additive-loaded packaged foods. Pure food is bursting with nutrients, each put to use in building and healing the body. Processed food is nutritionally bankrupt and associated with various health problems.

2. Stick to the Lean, Not to the Lard

In other words, gravitate toward low-fat foods. Of all nutrients, dietary fat seems to give us the most worry. This is because diets overloaded with fat (particularly animal fat) are implicated in the development of heart disease, cancer, and other life-shortening diseases. Also, too much dietary fat is easily converted to body fat. The more fat you eat, the more you're likely to wear. By a simple reduction in the amount of fat you consume, you can whittle away body fat and prevent weight-related illnesses.

START NOW!

Today, begin the 21-day plan by getting your nutritional house in order. Let the two nutritional principles described above be your guide, then start populating your diet with pure, low-fat foods .Also, refer to the appendix for information on how many serv-ings of each food you should have daily. Your body will love you for it.

Positive health changes begin right away. Within a week, your cholesterol profile will begin to improve. Concentrations of health-protective vitamins will increase in your blood. Your elimination will be better because you're eating more fiber. Plus, you'll have more pep than ever because of the volume of natural energy foods in your diet. And you'll start burning off excess body fat—automatically. All in one week!

Why such an amazing transformation in so little time? Because of the marvelous way God created food. Let's take a closer look at the categories of lean, pure food you should be eating and the health-building nutrients they contain.

LIFE-GIVING GRAINS

The book of Genesis recounts the time Jacob and his family endured a life-threatening famine in their homeland. Upon finding out there was food in Egypt, Jacob sent ten of his sons to buy some. He told them: "I have heard that there is grain in

Egypt. Go down there and buy some for us, so that we may live and not die" (Gen. 42:2).

Grain was considered vital to life, signifying its remarkable nutritional value. Grains such as wheat bran, oat bran, rice, oatmeal, cream of wheat, and bulgur wheat are "near-complete" foods because they contain protein, carbohydrates, and some essential fat. With fruits and vegetables, they are also a chief source of carbohydrate, the nutrient fuel on which our bodies run.

But the benefits don't stop there. Grains are loaded with a slew of trace minerals, including blood-building iron. Grains keep cholesterol levels in check and exert a protective effect on the body against cancer, particularly on the digestive system; they contain blood pressure–lowering nutrients such as potassium, and they are packed with B-complex vitamins, which are involved in metabolism (the sum of all physiological reactions necessary for life).

FRUITS AND VEGETABLES

Fruits and vegetables were the first foods God gave us. Their prime advantage is their abundance of special food factors— namely antioxidants and phytochemicals—both of which have many disease-fighting powers.

Antioxidants

Fruits and vegetables supply vitamins and minerals, two classes of nutrients vital to health. Several vitamins and minerals, namely beta carotene, vitamin C, vitamin E, and the mineral selenium, are known as "antioxidants." At the cellular level, antioxidants sweep up disease-causing substances known as "free radicals." Free radicals are volatile toxic molecules that cause harmful reactions in the body. In some cases, free radicals puncture cell membranes, preventing the intake of nutrients and thus starving the cells. In others, they tinker with the body's genetic material. This produces mutations that cause cells to act abnormally and reproduce uncontrollably. Scientists have linked some 60 diseases to free radicals. Among them heart disease, Alzheimer's disease, arthritis, and some cancers. Antioxidants guard against free radical damage and are thus health-protective. An antioxidant-rich diet affords significant health protection against these diseases.

It's best to get antioxidants from fruits and vegetables first, without relying totally on supplements. This is because of the way God created food. Scientists have recently discovered that antioxidants and other nutrients in fruits and vegetables work best as a team, rather than individually. That's why pure foods are best.

Still, you should take supplements as a nutritional insurance policy. Foods today are not as nutritious as they once were—a result of poor environmental stewardship. Modern farming methods, for example, have depleted the soil in many areas of the country, reducing the nutrients in food. Although God put us in charge of his creation, we haven't done a very good job of tending it, and the nutrient quality of our foods, among other things, has suffered. Taking a once-a-day antioxidant vitamin and mineral formula is a wise precaution, but make fruits and vegetables your primary source of antioxidants.

Phytochemicals

By eating lots of antioxidant-rich foods, you're automatically filling up on some newly discovered food factors with some amazing disease-fighting properties. They're called "phytochemicals," which means plant chemicals. Neither vitamins nor minerals, phytochemicals occur naturally in all fruits, vegetables, and grains. There are thousands of phytochemicals in foods (tomatoes contain 10,000), many yet to be discovered. They exert their health-protecting action by various biochemical mechanisms, and the results are amazing. Phytochemicals appear to protect against cancer, heart disease, and many other life-threatening illnesses.

To ensure you're getting enough antioxidants and phyto-chemicals, eat a variety of fruits and vegetables—in an assort-ment of colors. The more colorful a fruit or vegetable is, the higher its antioxidant and phytochemical content. Look at your dinner plate as a palette, painted with red, orange, yellow, and green vegetables. Praise the beauty of God's creation displayed in the rainbow of colors and abundance of nutrients in your foods.

FIBER FOR FITNESS

Found only in plant foods, fiber has an array of health benefits: It improves elimination, flushes cancer-causing substances from the system, and helps keep cholesterol levels in check by decreasing the absorption of dangerous cholesterol in the body.

A high-fiber diet will help you control your weight too—in several ways. Fiber makes you feel full, so you don't overeat. More energy (calories) is spent digesting and absorbing high-fiber foods. And fiber helps move food through your system more efficiently. This means fewer calories are left to be stored as fat. Natural foods such as whole grains, vegetables, and fruits are your best fiber bets.

LEAN PROTEINS: MEAT, FISH, POULTRY, AND DAIRY PRODUCTS

Responsible for building and maintaining body tissues, proteins are present everywhere in the body—in muscle, bones, connec-tive tissue, blood vessels, blood cells, skin, hair, and fingernails. These proteins are constantly being lost, or broken down, due to normal wear-and-tear on the body—and must be replaced by the food we eat. For example, about half of the total amount of pro-tein in muscle tissue is broken down and replaced every 150 days.

Protein is thus indispensable to life because it plays a role in every part of the body and in every cell. But protein—namely animal protein—has gotten a bad rap. It's been falsely accused of causing heart disease and other diet-related illnesses. The real villain in these conditions is saturated fat. The liver manufactures blood cholesterol from saturated fat. The more saturated fat you eat, the more cholesterol your liver makes. Excess cholesterol circulating in the bloodstream can collect in the inner walls of the arteries. This buildup is called "plaque," and it can lead to a heart attack.

To avoid such problems, eat animal protein that's low in saturated fat. Select lean proteins such as white-meat poultry, fish, and certain lean cuts of red meat (top round, top loin, round tip, tenderloin, sirloin, eye of round). Also, choose low-fat dairy products like skim milk and nonfat yogurt. These foods are also a rich source of bone-building calcium.

Additionally, animal proteins are the only food to supply vitamin B_{12}, vital for the healthy functioning of your nervous system. And your body absorbs iron and zinc better from animal sources than it does from plant foods. Thus it's critical to include animal protein in your diet.

FAT FACTS

Fat is one nutrient we all seem to fear, especially since it's linked to the top three causes of death in this country—heart disease, cancer, and stroke. Yet dietary fat is an essential nutrient, required to help form the structures of cell membranes, regulate metabolism, and provide a source of energy for exercise and activity.

The healthiest fats you can choose are vegetable oils. One of the most remarkable is olive oil, mentioned frequently in the Bible. A monounsaturated fat, olive oil has been scientifically proven to help improve blood cholesterol profiles, protect against heart attacks and strokes, strengthen cell membranes to guard against cell destruction, and provide a natural supply of the antioxidant vitamin E.

Nuts and seeds are also good sources of healthy fats. An excellent source of energy, they are also rich in vitamin E, fiber, protein, and minerals. A single Brazil nut is a treasure trove of selenium, an antioxidant mineral that may protect against cancer. But don't go nutty snacking on nuts. They're also a concentrated source of calories, so enjoy them in moderation. A tablespoon a day is enough to get their benefits.

As to how much fat to eat each day, here are some easy guidelines to follow:

- Use fats and oils sparingly in cooking and at the table.
- Use small amounts of salad dressings and spreads such as butter, margarine, and mayonnaise. Consider substituting low-fat or fat-free dressings on salads.
- Choose vegetable oils and soft margarines most often because they are lower in saturated fat than solid shortenings and animal fats.
- Use as little fat as possible to cook vegetables and grains.
- Season your foods with herbs, spices, lemon juice, and fat-free or low-fat salad dressings.

TO YOUR HEALTH!

These two simple principles will help you serve up a menu for a healthier life. Consult the appendix for information on exactly how much of these healthy foods you should eat daily.

LESSON OF THE DAY

Choose pure, low-fat foods that are as close
as possible to the way God created them.

DAY 2

The Most Important Health Move You Can Make Now

This Miracle Worker Could Disease-Proof Your Body

If you could bottle the benefits of exercise— which boosts your energy, makes you lose weight, bolsters your immune system, lifts depression, protects you from heart attacks, and even stretches out your active years—it would be the most prescribed medication in the world. There are piles of proof that exercise has more overall impact on your health than any other health action you can take. In 1996, the results of a landmark study were published comparing the effects of a sedentary lifestyle with other health risks. After following 32,000 people for eight years, the researchers discovered that those whose only health risk was inactivity were more apt to die prematurely than those with high cholesterol, high blood pressure, and a smoking habit but who exercised daily.

Sitting around, day in and day out, can be hazardous to your health.

God marvelously crafted the human body with 620 muscles that work together to move the 206 bones of the human skeleton. Because of this amazing design, our bodies can produce sufficient power to lift hundreds of pounds, yet most people rarely use all their muscles on a daily basis. As a result, muscles shrink and weaken, resulting in life-limiting illnesses that steal our vitality.

But this doesn't have to happen. The choice to exercise or not is yours.

Today, I want to walk you through several of the key benefits of exercise. However, I realize that merely understanding these benefits isn't enough to get you moving. So I want you to personalize them. For example, one benefit of exercise is that it's great for cardiovascular fitness. Okay, so what does that mean to you? Better reports on your physicals, year after year? Greater protection against heart disease, which runs in your family? Whatever the personal benefits, I want you to list them in the space provided. This exercise will transform "have to's" or "shoulds" into "want-to's." And this distinction can make all the difference in your journey to better health and fitness.

HEART HEALTH

Regular exercise protects against heart disease in a couple of important ways. First, it helps lower concentrations of dangerous fats in the blood, namely low-density lipoproteins (LDL). Lipoproteins are substances containing cholesterol, other blood fats, and protein. LDL is particularly harmful because it transports cholesterol from the blood into artery walls. The cholesterol forms artery-clogging plaque, narrowing the passageway and decreasing blood flow. Clogged arteries can cause a heart attack.

Researchers suspect that the action of a special fat-burning enzyme is accelerated with exercise. This results in a faster turnover of fat and consequently less fat buildup in the blood. With your blood fats in check, fatty deposits are less likely to accumulate inside your arteries.

Second, your heart becomes more efficient at doing its job, able to pump more blood with each beat, during exercise and while at rest. Your heart rate slows too, so when you climb stairs or do yard work, your heart doesn't have to work as hard.

Your entire circulatory system changes also. Exercise increases your capillaries in size and number, so more blood finds its way to the muscles and other tissues where it's needed to deliver nutrients and oxygen.

Personalize the benefit:

_____

_____

_____

FAT LOSS AND WEIGHT CONTROL

The real key to burning fat and keeping it off is exercise. One pound of body fat equals 3,500 calories. By burning 250 to 500 calories a day through exercise, you could lose up to a pound of fat a week (7 x 500 = 3,500)—without restricting food. Exercise also raises the metabolism and keeps it elevated for several hours afterward. The muscle you develop by exercising elevates your metabolism too. In fact, for every new pound of muscle you gain with exercise, you use about 50 to 100 calories more a day. You can eat more and not gain weight because you're burning more calories, even while sleeping.

Personalize the benefit:

_____

_____

_____

PROTECTION AGAINST CANCER

An emerging body of research suggests that exercise may cut the risk of some cancers, particularly cancers of the colon and breast. This is partly because obesity is a risk factor for cancer. Cancers of the uterus, gallbladder, breast, kidney, endometrium, and colon have all been linked to obesity. Because exercise, in conjunction with proper nutrition, fights obesity, it may serve as a protective factor against these cancers.

And several studies suggest that exercise can strengthen the immune system, a complex network of special cells, antibodies, and hormones that defend the body against disease. Many scientists thus theorize that a strong immune system can better stave off cancer.

Personalize the benefit:

_____

_____

_____

STRENGTH-BUILDING

Exercise physiologists estimate that, on average, you lose about seven pounds of muscle every decade after your mid-twenties— unless you remain active. This rate of loss accelerates after age forty-five. In addition to weakening your body, muscle loss is responsible for the slower metabolism blamed for mid-life weight gain. As your body loses muscle, it does not burn as many calories, and more fat is deposited. Over time, muscles tend to get stiffer, and connective tissues such as joints and ligaments weaken.

Exercise (particularly strength-developing exercise) prevents age-related muscle loss and builds strength. Stronger muscles increase flexibility, protect the joints, and ease the pain of arthritis.

Personalize the benefit:

_____

_____

_____

BONE DENSITY

As you age, your bones lose vital minerals, mainly bone-building calcium. This condition is called osteoporosis and results in brittle, fragile bones. In men, the loss of minerals can begin at about age fifty, but in women it can start as early as ages thirty to thirty-five. By age seventy, some women may lose up to 70 percent of their bone mineral mass. The good news is that weight-bearing exercise (strength training, running, walking, and so forth) offers protection against bone loss by stimulating the bone to produce new cells.

Personalize the benefit:

_____

_____

_____

BRAIN POWER

Exercise trains not only the body but also the mind. The neural processes controlling movement are slowed by age as brain cells shrink and messenger systems work less efficiently. One noticeable result is a reduction in reaction time—unless you exercise. People who regularly exercise are better able to keep their mental skills sharp. Researchers at the University of Utah compared the brain wave activity of two groups of older people, one very active, the other sedentary. They found that the brain waves of the active group more closely resembled those of younger people.

Personalize the benefit:

_____

_____

_____

PSYCHOLOGICAL FITNESS

Thousands of studies are showing that exercise is an effective remedy against many emotional problems of daily living. The strongest evidence suggests that exercise probably relieves symptoms of mild-to-moderate depression. There is also proof that exercise may complement counseling programs for alcoholism, substance abuse, and eating disorders; improve self-image and self-confidence; and alleviate symptoms of stress and anxiety. In short, exercise is a powerful way to improve mental health.

Exactly how this reaction occurs is still unclear, though research has shown that exercise releases certain chemicals produced by the brain, of which the most well-known are endorphins. These are responsible for reducing pain and heightening feelings of pleasure. The result is a general sense of mental well-being. Whenever regular exercisers are asked about the psychological benefits of working out, most say it makes them feel better, or they can handle stress better, or feel more energetic.

Personalize the benefit:

_____

_____

_____

QUALITY OF LIFE

God designed our bodies to move, yet as we get older, we tend to move them less. Therefore they lose function and mobility, making exercise harder and us less motivated to pursue it. Many of the physical problems we experience as we get older—heart trouble, osteoporosis, stiff joints, weaknesses, weight gain, and poor posture—are the result of inactivity. If you're out of shape physically, it can be difficult to follow Paul's advice in 1 Corinthians 15:58: "Always give yourselves fully to the work of the Lord, because you know that your labor in the Lord is not in vain." We're called to work fully for God. To do this, we need strength, energy, endurance, and good health.

Personalize the benefit:

GET MOVING!

Hopefully, you're convinced now that exercise has value for you. Incidentally, you may not need as much exercise as you think you do. Tomorrow, we'll look at how to sneak exercise into your day and how to find time for exercise.

LESSON OF THE DAY

God designed your body to move. Move it,
and you'll move closer to health and fitness.

DAY 3

Make Time for Exercise

Reclaim Your Schedule

Most people—research confirms this—say "lack of time" is their biggest obstacle to exercising. Truth be told, it's not that we don't have time, it's that *we need to better use the time we have*. There are 168 hours in one week. Shouldn't you be able to squeeze in at least three for exercise?

Absolutely. Today, take out your Daytimer, your calendar, or a plain note pad of paper. Start mapping out the days ahead—write in all the key activities, including appointments, errands, church activities, kids' activities, and so forth. As you do, you'll begin to see where your time goes each week. You'll identify free time slots you didn't know you had. Start scheduling exercise in those slots.

You'll be surprised to find that there's plenty of time for exercise.

EXERCISE IN DISGUISE

You may be exercising already and not even know it. Part of the reason 60 percent of

Americans don't exercise may be that they think "exercise" means a regimented, time-consuming program of vigorous activity. That's only part of it. In addition to structured activity, exercise includes recreational sports and lifestyle activities such as housework and yard work. In fact, painting, hanging wallpaper, and doing light carpentry provide the same metabolic results as walking at 3.5 mph (which is a pretty good clip). And gardening can burn as many as 500 calories an hour.

The key to improving fitness lies in getting a good balance of all these activities each week. So the question is: How much physical activity do you need weekly to make a difference?

Published in 1996, the first-ever U.S. Surgeon General's report on physical activity makes these important recommendations:

- Everyone older than age two should accumulate at least 30 minutes of endurance-type (aerobic) physical activity, of at least moderate intensity, most days of the week. Basically, this means you can accrue the recommended 30-minute minimum throughout the day—as opposed to a formal half-hour exercise session every day. The accrual can include a variety of activities. Thus, activities such as playing sports, mowing the lawn (on foot), housecleaning, climbing stairs instead of taking the elevator, or parking your car farther away and walking, can be counted toward the 30 minutes.

- You can achieve additional benefits by adding more time in moderate-intensity activity, or by substituting more vigorous activity. An example of "moderate" activity is walking briskly at three to four mph. Naturally, it's to your advantage to exercise longer and harder for greater fitness gains. Increasing duration and intensity should be done gradually.

- People with cardiovascular disease and other health problems who want to exercise should be examined by their physician and given an appropriate exercise program.

- Previously inactive men over age 40 and women over age 50, and people at high risk for cardiovascular disease, should first consult a physician before engaging in a program of vigorous exercise.
- Strength-developing activities should be performed at least twice a week, and should include one or two sets of 8 to 12 repetitions for the major muscle groups. These activities include working out with weights (dumbbells, barbells, and machines), exercising against the resistance of your own body (calisthenics), or using thick elastic bands.

You don't have to run a marathon or train for a triathlon to get fit. In fact, overexertion can tear down your body's resistance to disease. Many experts are now emphasizing a less-is-best approach to exercise. That's encouraging news if heretofore you thought you had to pursue a push-it-to-the-limit workout.

SOME TIME-SAVING EXERCISE TIPS

If you feel as though your leisure time has shrunk, leaving less time to exercise, here are several tips to help you beat the clock:

- *Squeeze in shorter workouts.* Try exercising in 10-minute bouts during the day. Researchers at Stanford University divided men into two groups: one group ran three times a day for 10 minutes each time and one group ran 30 minutes once a day. After eight weeks, both groups of exercisers had comparable fitness gains—in endurance and weight loss. Shorter workouts can do as much good as longer exercise sessions, and they're better than doing no exercise at all.
- *Start early.* Get up an hour or half hour earlier than you normally would and start exercising. (Have some fruit juice first for energy.) By working out early in the morning, you get your exercise session over with—and that

feels good. Plus, exercise will energize you mentally and physically for the rest of the day.

- *Work out at the office.* All across America, companies are setting up wellness programs for their employees, and many of these programs offer exercise facilities and classes. If your company has an on-site exercise program, take advantage of it—by working out before work, during your lunch hour, or after work.
- *Get help.* Friends and family are an important source of support as you pursue a healthier lifestyle. See if your spouse or another family member is willing to help you with a household task or watch the kids while you take time to exercise.

THE BOTTOM LINE

By identifying available time and realizing that you may already be getting a lot of physical activity, you should feel much better about committing to a more active lifestyle.

LESSON OF THE DAY

Make use of available time (at least thirty minutes most days) to exercise.

DAY 4

Fitness That Fits You

Excuse-Proof Your Fitness Program Forever

Perhaps you haven't yet discovered an exercise activity you can live with and love. You've tried a few things, but when they didn't interest you, you gave up.

Twenty years ago when I was trying to find an exercise I liked, the choices were limited. Calisthenics classes and sports were about the extent of it. Strength training for women was unheard of, and aerobic dance classes were in their infancy. There just weren't many choices.

Today all that has changed. In aerobic dance classes alone, you have numerous options, including classes like step, slide, high-impact, low-impact, crosstraining, and cardio-kick. Visit any large health club today and you'll see an array of exercise equipment, all with high-tech bells and whistles that make exercising fun and challenging. But if you prefer the low-tech, there's still good old-fashioned walking, which, according to the National Sporting Goods Association, is the number-one exercise activity in America.

SELECTING THE RIGHT EXERCISE

The point is, there are plenty of choices. The key is to pick the one, or ones, with the highest potential for making your lifestyle active for a lifetime. Today, analyze some basic criteria to consider when selecting the type of exercise that's right for you.

The Fun Factor

Too often, we start exercising because "it's good for us." So we tolerate it—not a good mind-set because eventually we'll terminate it. A better approach is to look for the "fun factor" in exercise. Remember when you were a kid? Weren't you active most of the time, climbing trees, playing ball, swimming? And wasn't it fun?

To make exercise a part of your life, it has to be fun—something that brings back the kid in you, or at least the spirit of enjoyment. When shopping around for an activity, look at the quality of the exercise experience. Ask yourself: Would it allow me to meet new people, learn new skills, engage in friendly competition? Would I do it for a lifetime? You really have to enjoy it that much.

Ability

Do you have the skills and abilities to perform certain exercises? Cross-country skiing might sound fun, but not if you lack the coordination to do it. Select exercises you can perform with a reasonable degree of skill. Your motivation multiplies when you know you can be successful. However, don't give up too easily as you experiment with different activities.

Convenience

Accessibility to pools, gyms, or tennis courts influences your decision to participate in certain activities. Studies show that one of the major reasons people drop out of exercise programs is inconvenience. It's easier to stick to your routine when exercise is convenient.

Affordability

Exercise ranges in price from the no cost to the high cost. Before committing, decide how much you can afford to invest in clothing, equipment, lessons, or gym memberships.

Personality

Consider how easily certain exercises match your personality. Do you like to work out alone or in the company of others? How structured or disciplined do you like your workouts to be? Are you competitive? Research shows that when your personality matches your exercise choice, motivation sharply increases.

LESSON OF THE DAY

Your chances of exercise success increase when you select activities based on enjoyment, lifestyle, and personality.

DAY 5

Keep-It-Simple Goal-Setting

The One-Step Formula for Guaranteed Success

Whenever I've been blessed with a book contract, I move quickly from celebration to panic. How will I ever be able to write an entire book? The thought of it overwhelms me—until I remember that a book is broken down into single chapters. I write one chapter at a time, and eventually the chapters become the book.

That's as it is with most successfully completed things in life. A building is built stone by stone. A race is won stride by stride. A picture is painted stroke by stroke. Early in a program to break bad habits, it's helpful to make daily, manageable resolutions, rather than to set and focus on far-off end goals. If all you do is concentrate on what you need to do today, achieving your end goal—like losing twenty pounds or fitting into those size 4 jeans—will take care of itself. Every day that's committed to achieving your resolutions will move you forward to the attainment of those greater goals.

Your daily resolutions should be easy to pull off. Each day, upon rising, resolve two things for the day: that you will eat good-for-you foods and do something active. Some examples of daily fitness resolutions might be:

"Cut my intake of sugary or fatty foods today."
"Drink one cup of coffee instead of three."
"Eat two extra servings of vegetables."
"Increase my endurance activity by 10 minutes."
"Play an active game with my kids."
"Learn a new strength-developing exercise."
"Use the stairs instead of an elevator or escalator."

Ask yourself today: What can I do to improve my nutrition and become more active? Then formulate your daily resolution and go for it. Continue to do this every day. Before long, you'll be sliding into those jeans, or buckling your belt a lot tighter.

It may also help to tie your daily fitness resolutions to your daily routine. There are things you routinely do each day, like going to work or putting your child down for a nap. Associate daily tasks with a daily activity goal. For example, make it routine to exercise after you finish work. Thus, your new routine becomes: leave work—go to the gym. This technique is a great way to form new health habits.

The important principle is to adopt a just-for-today attitude. Jesus says, "Therefore do not worry about tomorrow, for tomorrow will worry about itself. Each day has enough trouble of its own" (Matt. 6:34). God wants us to live one day at a time, trusting him to take care of our future needs.

Just before Moses parted the Red Sea, the Israelites saw the Egyptians coming after them. Understandably, they were afraid, and wisely, they cried out to the Lord. Yet they complained to Moses that bondage in Egypt had to be better than death in the desert. Moses reassured them in a way that speaks to us now, whatever our situation: "Do not be afraid. Stand firm and you will see the deliverance the Lord will bring you today. The Egyptians you see today you will never see again. The LORD will fight for you; you need only to be still" (Ex. 14:13–14).

Sometimes it feels more comfortable to be in the bondage of our old habits. They tug at us, but we know that giving in to them will only hurt us in the long run. Parting with the old habits in order to make way for the new takes a firm, abiding belief in God's guidance. We can take comfort in knowing that we never have to experience those old habits again. Notice Moses used the word *today*, not *tomorrow* or *next month*. God can deliver you from the bondage of bad habits today.

Above all, keep God in any resolutions or goals you set. Proverbs 16:3 says, "Commit to the Lord whatever you do, and your plans will succeed." When Peter and the disciples went fishing one night, they caught nothing (John 21:1–6). The next morning, Jesus appeared to them on the shore. He told them to cast their net on the other side of the boat. When they did, their net was so full they could barely haul in the catch. Without God, our efforts are fruitless. But with divine help and direction, our efforts never fail.

LESSON OF THE DAY

Make healthy choices just for today and keep God at the center of your plans.

DAY 6

Willpower Has Nothing to Do with It

How to Zap Fitness Failure Once and for All

When I was a junior in college, I embarked on my first "diet." I enrolled in a well-known weight-loss program, followed it religiously, and in four months lost twenty-two pounds. I looked terrific. Friends and family showered me with compliments.

Home from college in the summer, I got a job in a restaurant as a food preparer and hostess. I found myself surrounded by food I had denied myself while following the diet: cheesecake, parfaits, ice cream. Alone in the restaurant by day, I started gobbling up servings of the cheesecake I was to slice for customers. Overcome by guilt and remorse, I panicked—the gorging could make me fat again. What would people think if I regained this weight? Not wanting to face that sentence, I shielded myself inside a bathroom stall, stuck my finger down my throat, and threw up. Disgusted, I vowed this would be the last time I'd eat the restaurant's cheesecake or any other forbidden food. Nor would I ever again make myself vomit. But that one-time gorge-purge episode turned into an 11-year struggle with bulimia, a life-threatening eating disorder.

Also during this period, I became "addicted" to diet programs; I felt that if I wasn't a paying member of some kind of weight-loss group, I was hopelessly on my own, with no chance of success. Once, I was in three diet programs at the same time!

When it finally hit me that I was committing slow suicide, I just gave up. I don't mean I gave up hope; I gave up dieting, bingeing, purging, joining weight-loss groups, and the like.

Sometimes, but not always, you come face-to-face with the terrifying reality that your behavior is killing you. Fear—the one emotion with real survival value—takes over and you decide to change. Your turning point may be survival too. Or it might be vanity, or something else. The important thing is that you want to break unhealthy habits and change your lifestyle for the better.

FORGET WILLPOWER

At that crucial turning point, you might say: "This time I'll do it because I've got willpower." Boy, are you in for a fall.

Willpower. That knuckle-down, do-it-or-die kind of determination. Let me personify it for you. Meet Will Power. When he's around, you're a good person. Strong enough to stick to your program, resist temptation, accomplish your goals. It sure is a great feeling to have Will Power. But after a few days he cuts out, and you feel like a failure. You're nothing without Will Power, except lazy and weak. The whole experience of trying to diet, exercise, or kick a bad habit is a real bummer. Why even try again?

Today, I want you to forget willpower and begin to see that you have something better.

SPIRITUAL STEPS TO LASTING CHANGE

The relapses we seem to experience over and over again are proof that willpower has never been enough to help us succeed.

The latest statistics on health behaviors reveal that nearly two-thirds of American adults are sedentary, and 90 percent of those who go on diets regain the weight, plus interest, within five years. Despite the billions of dollars spent to prevent and treat it, obesity among adults in the United States rose from 25 percent in 1980 to 34 percent today. Medical experts chalk the obesity problem up to the typical American diet, which continues to be high in fat and sugar and low in fiber. Also, people are eating more. In the last 10 years, calorie intake has increased by 100 to 300 calories a day, and those calories are probably coming from the high-fat, high-sugar stuff.

At present, "behavioral self-management techniques" (a fancy name for willpower-based programs) are considered the best way to treat weight problems. This approach focuses on changing behavior patterns to increase exercise and decrease calories. But according to an article by two noted nutrition and obesity experts in the *Journal of the American Dietetic Association*, this approach isn't working. People with a weight problem who try to exert self-control just can't seem to stick to their programs. Mounds of research provide evidence that programs requiring the self-control of participants just don't work very well.

Sticking to a program of change requires a new approach, one that doesn't rely so much on self. The first step to lasting change is to submit your will to God's—in other words, surrender. Wave the white flag and tell God you need help.

You can't surrender unless you decide to—and that, in a sense, is willpower. So I don't want to be too hard on ol' Will Power. Willpower does point you in the right direction, so in itself it isn't bad. After all, God gives us the freedom to choose. But our willpower is best exercised in choosing to surrender to his power. When we let go of a situation we can't control and put it into God's hands, we find his power is all we need.

Remember when Jesus fed the 5,000 (John 6:5–13)? Now there was a problem—a throng of people to feed and no food. So the Lord asked his disciple Philip, "Where shall we buy bread for these people to eat?" The question was only a test, for Jesus already had a plan. Philip gave the excuse that they couldn't afford to feed all those people, while Andrew, another disciple, went looking for food. He found a little boy with only five barley loaves and two tiny fish—still not enough, still a problem. But the little boy put the problem in the Lord's hands, and it was the making of a miracle. The Lord multiplied the meager provisions and fed every person there. When you've got a problem, like a nagging bad habit, God will give you what you need to change it—maybe even beyond your wildest expectations. Just put it in his hands. He already has a plan to solve your problem.

Not only that, God has endowed you with spiritual resources to help you see it through. When you put your trust in Christ, God sends his Holy Spirit to live inside you to begin a work of reconstruction, a work that involves building Christ's character in you. This character-building process ripens, producing in you the fruit of the Spirit listed in Galatians 5:22–23: love, joy, peace, patience, kindness, goodness, faithfulness, gentleness, and self-control.

It should encourage you to know that you already have self-control—the power to control your will under the operation of the Holy Spirit and use it to make Christ-honoring choices. As long as you follow Christ's leading each day, your life will begin to more fully display self-control, along with other Christlike virtues.

LESSON OF THE DAY

You have everything necessary to choose healthy behavior—a choice that is God's will for your life. However tough it has been up until now, God's power will see you through.

DAY 7

On the Seventh Day, Rest

The Rejuvenating Power of Doing Nothing

Is yours an on-the-go lifestyle—sometimes exciting but often exhausting? If so, it's time to talk about something that's as essential to fitness as nutrition and exercise: rest.

Rest lets your body renew itself. During this renewal, the body can heal injuries and infections, eliminate toxins and waste products, dissipate stress, replenish fuel stores in your muscle fibers and bloodstream, and restore energy. Rest also allows your immune system to recharge so you're better protected from disease.

Sleep, in particular, revives you mentally and physically. It improves your productivity and creativity and restores your brain function, including information processing. During sleep, the repair of all body tissues takes place and disease-fighting systems are bolstered.

Rest is an absolute requirement for physical and spiritual refreshment. God showed us this principle when he rested on the seventh day of creation. He then commanded us to take a weekly vacation called the Sabbath (Exod.

Is Sound Sleep Only a Dream?

Researchers who study the lifestyles of people who stay healthy well into their golden years have identified these seven health habits shared by the fit:

- Eating regular meals
- Eating breakfast every day
- Maintaining a healthy body weight
- Avoiding excessive alcohol consumption
- Exercising regularly
- Not smoking
- Sleeping seven to eight hours a night

Notice the last item on the list. Restful sleep is a critical component of health and fitness. Yet, health experts believe that sleep deprivation has become one of the most pervasive health problems in the United States, responsible for personality disorders, traffic accidents, debilitating fatigue, memory loss, decreased physical performance, and illness.

To get and stay fit, you must get sound shut-eye. Sleep is as critical to the body as exercise and nutrition because it gives your body time to recover and revive. You know you've had a restful night when you can wake up without your alarm clock and feel refreshed the rest of the day. If you're having trouble achieving that kind of slumber, here are some practical tips:

- Don't exercise too late in the day or in the evening.
- Go to bed at a regular time and maintain a regular sleep schedule.
- Darken your room and keep it well-ventilated.
- Avoid caffeine and alcohol. Eliminate caffeine after midday.
- Make sure your mattress is supportive and comfortable.
- Create a neat, restful sleep environment.
- Pray to God before you go to sleep at night—or meditate on Scripture.

For those who make the right choices in life—God-honoring choices—God says that "when you lie down, you will not be afraid; when you lie down, your sleep will be sweet" (Prov. 3:24). How wonderful—the comfort of falling into a pleasant slumber, free from those anxious thoughts that keep us tossing and turning all night. Keep God's ways and apply his truths to your life daily and you can sleep like a baby.

20:8), which is meant to be a day set aside for rest and worship. For the nation of Israel, the Sabbath was Saturday on the Jewish calendar, in commemoration of the end of six days of work; for Christians, it is Sunday (the Lord's Day), in commemoration of the day Christ rose from the dead.

Keeping a "sabbath"—which means to cease activity—is a God-given escape hatch from burnout, stress, workaholism, and the life-and-spirit damage these behaviors bring. Our bodies and spirit were simply not meant to work day after day without rest. If you continue to work without rest, sooner or later your body will go on strike and get sick. You'll be *forced* to rest.

We need a schedule punctuated by a seventh day of rest. During World War II, Great Britain instituted a 74-hour workweek but discovered that workers couldn't maintain a productive pace. The government switched to a 48-hour workweek, with regular breaks, plus one day of rest each week. The new work schedule resulted in maximum productivity. There's a great saying that puts this all in perspective: Seven days make one weak.

God wants us to rest every seven days. To apply this principle to your life, arrange your schedule so that after six days of work, you rest. Forget about your work, bills, or other obligations. Just rest. This may mean reading a good book, watching an old movie, going on a family picnic, taking a nap—anything that gets you away from your everyday work routine. Whatever relaxes, unwinds, and recharges—do it!

Even more important, this day should bring spiritual refreshment to strengthen you for the week ahead. For most people, the seventh day is Sunday, a day set apart to worship and serve God. Just think of all the God-honoring acts Jesus did on the Sabbath: He healed the sick, taught in the synagogue, read God's Word, fed himself and his disciples when hungry, restored a man's sight, released a woman from Satan's bondage, and more. Exciting things can happen on this special day when you devote yourself to the Lord.

So ask yourself, How can I best serve God today, bring him honor, and grow closer to him? You might start this day by reading Psalm 92, "A Song for the Sabbath Day," which was used in temple services on the Sabbath.

LESSON OF THE DAY

For physical and spiritual health,
your body needs to rest every seventh day.
Take that rest, beginning this week.

Fitness Saboteurs

The 5 Best Ways to Turn Them into Supporters

It could be your spouse, your mother, your best friend. They know you're trying to eat right and exercise regularly. But then comes the pound of chocolate candy on Valentine's Day . . . the carry-out pizza with everything on it . . . the invitation to an all-you-can-eat pancake breakfast. How can you stick to your fitness commitment when surrounded by "saboteurs"—people who knowingly or unknowingly may be undermining your fitness efforts?

Today, you'll equip yourself with some practical tips for handling saboteurs and turning them into supporters. And you'll find these tips in Daniel 1:8–17. The scene is King Nebuchadnezzar's court in Babylon following his attack on Jerusalem. Nebuchadnezzar has ordered his chief official to select several young Jewish men who are physically fit and mentally bright to be educated in the king's palace for three years and then enter his personal service. Among the youths chosen were Daniel, Hananiah, Mishael, and Azariah.

The king ordered that the youths be fed his food and wine—a diet that probably included forbidden meats and thus violated God's dietary laws. Additionally, the first portion of the food may have been sacrificed to idols and the first portion of the wine poured over pagan altars—in further violation of God's laws.

Resolved not to pollute his body with the royal food, Daniel asked the officials to let them eat only vegetables and drink only water. This was a very good diet compared to the king's menu, which was probably high in fat and dehydrating because of the alcohol. The all-vegetable fare was high in carbohydrates, vitamins, minerals, fiber, and phytochemicals—a wonderful nutritional prescription for great health. Water is necessary for growth, development, and health.

Nonetheless, the officials feared that the boys' health would suffer, while the chief official feared that the king would have his head (literally). But Daniel talked them into a ten-day trial. Not only did the youths survive on the vegetarian diet, they thrived on it. After ten days, they were much healthier than the youths who had eaten the king's food.

There's much to learn from this story in terms of dealing with saboteurs and turning them into supporters. Here are some guidelines:

- *Set your heart on following a healthy lifestyle.* When the Scripture says that Daniel resolved not to defile himself, it's describing a deep, heartfelt commitment. In fact, the literal translation of *resolved* is "set his heart upon." It's not enough to make up your mind about something; you must set your heart on what you want to accomplish—a deep-down desire to do what's right. Daniel's heartfelt commitment was to obey God—as ours should be. God desires that we choose healthy behaviors even when those around us want to change our lifestyle. A heartfelt commitment, born out of loving obedience to God, will see you through.

- *Plan ahead.* Before they even saw the king's spread of food, Daniel and his friends decided not to partake. It's easier to stick to a healthy course of action if you decide to do so before the situation or saboteurs present themselves. My husband and I practice this principle often. If we're trying to improve our diets, or shed a few pounds, we agree before we go to a party or event that we will not eat things that could compromise our goal. Preplanning works much better than merely throwing caution to the wind.

- *Be gracious in compromising circumstances.* Daniel doesn't make a big to-do about sticking to his diet or demand that the court serve things his way. Instead, *he asks the chief official for permission* not to eat the king's food—a humble, gracious request. Daniel's example is an admirable one for us to emulate. Suppose you're on a special diet for health reasons but invited to an event where all the wrong foods will be served. Graciously ask permission to bring some of your own food, or politely explain to your host or hostess your reasons for not eating certain foods.

- *Understand the saboteur's position.* Some saboteurs may feel threatened by your decision to get in shape. A good example is the wife who loses a lot of weight. Her husband frets over whether he'll lose her to another man and so tries to fatten her up again. To him, life is more secure lived in the old patterns. The court official in the story of Daniel was afraid of losing his life if he let Daniel stay on his diet. The feeling of being threatened is very real. So is jealousy. Your best friend might feel jealous over your success at losing weight—a feeling that drives a wedge in your relationship. Granted, these emotions are not your problem, and you should not change your course to win the approval of others. But you must be sensitive to their feelings, particularly those of a spouse or close friend. The best strategy is to turn the saboteur into a supporter. How? Read on.

- *Negotiate rather than rebel.* Rather than pitch a fit, Daniel negotiated an experimental ten-day vegetarian diet—a practical, doable contract. The experiment resulted in a win-win situation for everyone. The four youths "looked healthier and better nourished than any of the young men who ate the royal food" (v. 15). The positive results won over the officials, who took away the royal food and let Daniel and his friends eat vegetables instead. Daniel turned the saboteurs into supporters.

Try a similar approach. Invite your spouse, friend, or family member to try exercising, or a new healthy food, just for a trial period. Your invitation might go something like this: (To your spouse): "I want to spend more time with you because I love being together. Let's try an exercise program together, just for two weeks, to see how we like it. Wouldn't that be a great opportunity to be together more often?" (To a friend or loved one): "I'd like to stay in touch with you more often. Why don't we join an exercise class, or walk together in the morning, to keep each other motivated?"

By sharing the experience with a partner, you can help each other stay motivated. Partners encourage one another to move from unhealthy to healthy behaviors. One study found that women who work out with their husbands are more likely to stick to fitness programs than married women who exercise alone. Another found that men are three times as likely to stay on a healthy diet if their wives encourage them to do so. As Solomon writes in Ecclesiastes 4:9–10: "Two are better than one, because they have a good return for their work: If one falls down, his friend can help him up."

Be loving, supportive, and encouraging. Follow Paul's advice about encouragement: "Encourage one another and build each other up" (1 Thess. 5:11). Give your partner frequent pats on the back with encouraging words like "You look terrific" or "You can do it."

Sharing the fitness experience gives you both something new to talk about together, and better communication, especially in marriage, is always a source of greater closeness. At the end of the trial period, give your partner some type of fitness gift, such as a new warm-up suit or gift certificate for athletic shoes. By that time, hopefully, your partner will want to join you in continuing this powerful new lifestyle.

No matter how it turns out, be a fitness witness. When you change right before people's eyes, it can inspire them to improve their own lives. Following the example of Daniel, resist compromise. Keep your commitment to developing a fit lifestyle. If your spouse or loved ones see consistency in your life, they're more likely to follow in your footsteps. The courage of Daniel's convictions certainly made an impact on the Babylonian official. But behind the scenes, God changed the official's heart. While we may pave the way, change ultimately comes from God.

LESSON OF THE DAY

Your personal commitment and conviction
can inspire others to follow your path.

Talk Yourself into Good Habits

Innermost Conversations That Can Transform Your Lifestyle

Consultant and author Glenn van Ekeren writes:

Have you ever seen the breathtaking pillars in Mammoth Cave in Kentucky? These solid, enormous "icicles of stone" have taken centuries to form. A single drop of water finds its way through the roof of the cavern to deposit its tiny sediment on the floor of the cave. Another drop follows, and still another, until a marble-like finger begins to grow. Ultimately, this process forms a tremendous pillar.

A similar process goes on in each of us. Each of our thoughts sinks into our soul, inadvertently forming our own pillars—pillars of character. If we let dishonest, immoral, selfish, and violent thoughts constantly fill our minds, we will form decaying pillars of weakness and evil. If we fill our minds with ideas, truth, love, and sincerity, we build strong and beautiful pillars within our souls. For it is the sum total of our daily thoughts that paint the portrait of our true character.[1]

Psychologists call this inner conversation "self-talk." But it's not some new, whiz-bang therapeutic technique; it's a bonafide biblical principle. Solomon summed it up best: "For as he thinks within himself, so he is" (Prov. 23:7 NASB).

Inner conversations can have a powerful impact on motivation and well-being. What you think determines what you say, what you do, and how you act. The more affirming your self-talk, the more successful you'll be at banishing destructive bad habits. You can learn how to slip out of self-defeating thoughts with a few simple techniques—techniques that can help you crystallize your new fitness habits and vitalize your health.

EAVESDROP ON YOUR SELF-TALK

Have you ever really listened to your self-talk? More often than not, inner conversation tends to be negative, and that's one reason why attempts at getting in shape sometimes fail. Negative self-talk is sabotaging; it can leave you feeling immobilized, helpless, and hopeless.

Here are some examples of what people tell themselves regarding their personal fitness:

"I'm too flabby to go to the pool."
"I'll never lose weight."
"I hate exercising."
"I'm disgusted with my appearance."
"I can't stick to a diet."
"I missed a few exercise classes. I'll just quit."

Sound familiar? Maybe it's time to course-correct by fighting your negative self-talk. The first step is to . . .

REWRITE YOUR INTERNAL SCRIPT

Paul says in Philippians 4:8: "Whatever is true, whatever is noble, whatever is right, whatever is pure, whatever is lovely, whatever is admirable—if anything is excellent or praiseworthy—think about such things." A beautiful description of positive self-talk, this passage lists six points that should be the focus of our careful reflection—points that can be applied to any area of life, including health and fitness:

1. Whatever Is True

Once you realize what your negative thoughts are, decipher whether there's any truth in them. Much of the stuff we tell ourselves about ourselves is a distortion of the truth, or not truthful at all. Suppose you say to yourself, "I'm a total failure because I can't lose weight." That's a lie. Surely, you've had plenty of successes in your life, so there's no way you can be a "total failure." And losing weight or not isn't an accurate yardstick of success or failure.

After dissecting your self-talk and challenging its truthfulness, replace the untruth with true, logical statements about yourself. Using the example above, you might tell yourself: "I'm not a failure. My commitment to changing my lifestyle is a sign of success. Every time I make even one healthy choice, I am succeeding."

2. Whatever Is Noble

"Noble" subjects are those that deserve our respect, and certainly one of these is our health. Thus, one focus of your self-talk should be the positive actions you're taking now, the things you're working on, and the ways you're getting healthier as a result.

3. Whatever Is Right

We often spend too much time thinking about our setbacks. If you look at all your unsuccessful attempts to get in shape as failures, you're bound to repeat your stop/start patterns of exercise. Instead, congratulate yourself for all the times you've tried. Along the way, you probably discovered many types of exercise or diets that didn't work for you, because you didn't enjoy them, you physically couldn't perform them, or in the case of a diet, it was too restrictive. Thomas Edison was once asked about his many failures in his search for a new storage battery—50,000 experiments before he achieved results. "Results?" replied the inventor. "Why, I have gotten results. I know 50,000 things that won't work."

So try thinking about those positive things you're doing now to become the person you were meant to be.

4. Whatever Is Pure

Your thought life can be easily polluted with negative words like *can't*, *never*, or *won't*; or put-downs, self-blaming, and other derogatory statements. A steady stream of pollution can lead to self-doubt, anxiety, and ultimately, depression. Pure thoughts are can-do/will-do inner conversations that build up rather than put down. The result can be a renewed, more upbeat attitude toward life.

5. Whatever Is Lovely

One of the best prescriptions for what ails you may be good thoughts. According to the Bible, your self-talk can make you disease-prone or health-prone, and a growing body of research supports this: "Pleasant words are a honeycomb, sweet to the soul and healing to the bones" (Prov. 16:24). Every snippet of self-talk can affect your body in some way. So fill yourself with "lovely" self-talk—messages that are pleasing, encouraging, nurturing, and loving.

6. Whatever Is Admirable

When you admire something, you hold it in very high regard. Yet seldom do we esteem or acknowledge our admirable qualities, preferring instead to dwell on where we fall short. And we come away from this self-criticism feeling inadequate and depressed.

One powerful scriptural truth with the potential to put such negativity to rest is this: Humans were made in God's image. "God created man in his own image, in the image of God he created him; male and female he created them" (Gen. 1:27). This image includes a character likeness, reflecting God's love, goodness, and faithfulness. The fact that you resemble God in certain traits should make you feel positive about yourself. Maligning yourself is finding fault with what God has created and the gifts he has given you. The fact that you were made by God in his image means you are valuable and worthwhile.

MOVE FROM SELF-DEFEAT TO PERSONAL VICTORY

One of the best ways to do this is to make a list of your typical negative messages, or "defeatist statements," and replace those messages with flip-side positive messages, or "victory statements." Here are some examples:

Defeatist Statement	Victory Statement
I can't change.	God can change me. My life is in his care.
I'm a couch potato.	I used to be inactive, but now I'm exercising.
I've tried and I always fail.	I don't always fail. Every healthy choice I make is a major success.
I'm uncoordinated.	I'm physically strong because I exercise. And I choose low-pressure exercises matched to my skill level.

I'm too fat.	Every moment I exercise and eat right, my body is becoming more efficient at burning fat for fuel.
I'm not very athletic.	Regular exercise makes me feel like an athlete.

NOW IT'S YOUR TURN

Replace your defeatist statements with victory statements. Begin to reshape your thought patterns and ultimately pull yourself out of the negative self-talk rut.

My Defeatist Statements	My Victory Statements
_____	_____
_____	_____
_____	_____
_____	_____
_____	_____

FINALLY, GET IN THE LAST WORD

What you think about before you go to bed can determine your course of action the next day. In Micah 2:1, God issues this warning: "Woe to those who plan iniquity, to those who plot evil on their beds! At morning's light they carry it out because it is in their power to do it."

As you lie down to sleep each night, think about all the positive changes you're making in your lifestyle and how they're vitalizing your health. Or try meditating on passages of Scripture that have strengthened you thus far. Your staying power the next day, as well as each successive day, will be a snap.

Your thoughts determine your actions and can affect your personal well-being. You were created in God's image; don't downgrade what he has made.

Warning—Bumpy Road Ahead

The Anti-Rut Plan of Action

There are bumps along the road to fitness, but they don't have to mean a permanent roadblock to a fit lifestyle. You can bridge over them. Today, let's look at how.

BUMP: IMMEDIATE GRATIFICATION

Do you want visible changes overnight, or the fastest results with the least effort? That's the essence of immediate gratification. Suppose you decide to start exercising but with one goal in mind: "instant fitness" in the form of weight loss or muscle tone. When the results don't come fast enough, you get discouraged, lose enthusiasm, and before long, another attempt to get in shape bites the dust. The immediate-gratification bump turns into a roadblock.

Bridge:

Outward results from exercise and proper nutrition are not instant, so it's best to scale back your sky-high expectations. Don't hold your new fitness program hostage to what you look like on the outside. Instead, refocus: Begin to associate exercise and nutrition with other down-the-road benefits such as better sleep, more energy, mental alertness, or reduced risk of disease.

To many people, the early stages of habit change are pure drudgery. But remember: In only 21 days, new habits can become automatic. Scripture says, "The end of a matter is better than its beginning" (Ecc. 7:8). In the back of your mind, remember what you have to look forward to: a time when good fitness habits are second nature.

BUMP: UNFIT FOR FITNESS

I've met many people (mainly women) over the years who are too self-conscious about their bodies to go to a health club or join an exercise class, so they just stay home and do nothing. They think their figures are less-than-perfect and don't dare to be seen in leotards or gym shorts.

The way you think and feel about your appearance is your body image. If you're like most people, your body image is constantly under attack—mainly by you. Somehow, you're never quite content with your looks, your size, or your shape. By improving your appearance and lifting your mental outlook, a fit, active lifestyle will free you from these harmful dissatisfactions. You'll develop a renewed appreciation for yourself, for how you look and feel, and for what you can accomplish.

Bridge:

Don't let your present body image immobilize you. I guarantee this: Enter the doors of any health club in this nation, and you'll see all shapes and sizes. As for people staring at you, forget it! Most exercisers are thrilled to see other people, regardless of their present condition, get into the fitness act and try to improve themselves. Not only that, the real die-hard exercisers are so into their workouts that they don't pay any attention to anyone else—unless, of course, you accidentally drop a dumbbell on their toe.

When you join a health club or an exercise class, you meet new people and develop new circles of friends, and you join a fellowship of those who are committed to a fitness lifestyle—a camaraderie that helps boost your commitment. In the first experiment ever conducted in social psychology (1897), a researcher had children wind fishing reels. The kids performed faster when another child was present than when alone. The result was not simply the result of competition, either. Other studies have found that performance improves by the mere presence of people engaged in the same behavior but not interacting or competing—much like you'd find in a gym or health club setting.

Still not convinced? Exercise at home on a regular basis until you feel confident to join a health club. The privacy factor of working out at home is appealing. If you don't like the way you look in gym clothes, no one has to see you exercising at home. You can concentrate on reshaping your body without feeling inhibited. Consider using exercise videos, working out on aerobic equipment such as a stationary bicycle or treadmill, or purchasing an inexpensive home weight-training gym.

Be aware that home exercisers have a tougher time being faithful to their routines. You don't have the motivation that working out in the presence of others can provide. So if you're on your own, you need other motivators. For example, find a picture of a person whose body you admire—someone with a bone structure similar to yours—and pin it up where you can see it while you're working out. Then imagine yourself looking like that person.

BUMP: BOREDOM

Maybe you've found it easy to begin an exercise program. But staying with it has been another story altogether. Your problem is typical: boredom. When that sets in, dropping out of exercise is not far behind.

Bridge:

If you're feeling bored already, start mixing up your exercise routine. Some ideas:

- Try a sport instead of conventional exercise.
- Branch out to forms of exercise you haven't tried before.
- Change the sequence and type of exercises in your routine.
- Participate in fitness contests sponsored by your health club.
- Set up your own competition. For example, certain types of aerobic exercise equipment let you race against a computerized competitor.

Variety is important not only mentally but physically. By changing your workouts, you can achieve additional fitness gains. (On Day 12, you'll learn more about how to make exercise stick, with some "exercise booster shots.")

BUMP: BUSYNESS

An interruption in your schedule—particularly a busy week— can put your exercise session on the back burner. And that's okay. But don't let it stay there. Oftentimes, one little miss in exercise can lead to huge lapses, and then to a permanent layoff.

Bridge:

Anytime you're thinking about skipping your exercise session, whip out this list and remind yourself of what can happen if you stop exercising regularly:

- Muscles decrease in size, tone, and strength.
- The activity of fat-burning enzymes declines.
- Your muscles lose their ability to store energy-yielding glycogen.
- The heart becomes deconditioned, and your body's aerobic power declines.

- The heart and lungs become less efficient.
- You lose speed and flexibility.
- Body fat gradually returns, and fat cells enlarge.

BUMP: PAST HISTORY

This bump can derail the possibility of ever having a healthy lifestyle. It appears on the road when you decide, based on your past failures, that it's impossible to stick to a fitness program. Maybe you were unathletic as a child. Have you transferred that feeling into adulthood? If so, you probably have a negative estimate of your physical capabilities. Though you might have been a klutz at sports in school, there are plenty of exercises that require no coordination at all, such as walking or strength training.

Bridge:

Stop looking in the rearview mirror: Past history should not be an indicator of future performance. Think of your previous attempts as experiments that are moving you closer to a time when eating right and exercising regularly are no longer a struggle but a permanent part of your lifestyle.

It may reassure you to know that change takes place in an erratic way. Your track record will show a few false starts, along with some sustained runs. If you're not prepared for the false starts, you'll panic and want to give up. As long as you're aware that you'll have setbacks, you'll be easier on yourself. Remember, progress is built on perseverance, one day at a time. Although Babe Ruth once had the most home runs on record, he also struck out 1,331 times.

BUMP: ILLNESS OR INJURY

It happens to the best of us: an illness or injury. It could be a bad cold, the flu, a backache, pulled muscle, or broken bone.

Depending on its severity, you could be sidelined for a while. There goes your exercise program, but don't despair. It's not advisable to work out when you're sick or injured, because exercise can aggravate the condition. But don't let your nutrition go down the tubes. You need proper nutrition, now more than ever.

Bridge:

Continue to make healthy food choices, since nutrients can help you stay on the mend when out of commission. But if you're not exercising, you may need to reduce your calories slightly by reducing your portions a bit. Make sure to eat plenty of grains, vegetables, and fruits since these supply many of the nutrients your body needs for healing. Plus, they help prevent constipation caused by bed rest or inactivity.

Don't forgo lean proteins, since they are essential for rebuilding body tissue. When you're injured, your body immediately starts breaking down muscle protein to provide the energy required to repair damaged tissues. So without adequate protein in your diet, your rate of healing could slow down to less than what's considered its normal rate.

The best medicine right now is to stay in prayer over your condition (see Day 18), follow your physician's orders, get the rest you need, and continue to eat properly.

THE ULTIMATE BRIDGE

David writes in Psalm 37:23–24, "If the Lord delights in a man's way, he makes his steps firm; though he stumble, he will not fall, for the Lord upholds him with his hand." When you're trying your best to make the right choices in life, God will steady your steps. Sure, you might backslide here and there, but it's not the end of the road. God is there to pick you up, hold your hand, and lead you forward, stronger than ever.

LESSON OF THE DAY

Knowing where the bumps are on the road to fitness can help you bridge over to healthy habits.

DAY 11

When Your Pep Is Pooped

Instant Energizers That Erase Fatigue

Some days, it may be all you can do to drag yourself out of bed, let alone get to the gym for a workout. Could it be you're having an energy crisis?

You're just about halfway through your 21 days to better fitness. Today, it's time to do an energy check to make sure you're powered for performance. Analyze some of your other health habits to see what could be making you feel draggy.

ARE YOU SKIPPING BREAKFAST?

Your mother always told you: Breakfast is the most important meal of the day. And she was right. Skipping breakfast leads to food cravings later, intense hunger, and low energy. You wake up each morning after an all-night fast; it's not fair to your health to continue that fast well into the day. Your body needs wholesome food in the morning to re-energize. The best breakfast is one that's well-rounded, with some protein (skim milk, soy milk, yogurt, eggs or egg whites, or low-fat cheese), plus some complex carbohydrates such as whole-grain cereals and fruits. These foods provide the fuels you need to get going in the morning. One reason people don't eat a good breakfast is lack of time. So you'll never go hungry in the morning, try my suggestions for two-minute blender breakfasts explained on page 76.

IS YOUR DIET MAKING YOU DRAG?

Excess sugar and fat in just a single meal can make you so sluggish you want to crawl under the covers for hours. Each year, the average American consumes 120 pounds of sugar—a 1,000 percent increase from a century ago when people ate between 10 and 20 pounds a year.

Sugar and sugary foods produce an instant rush of energy, which is followed by a fast drop in blood sugar. When blood sugar declines, you feel tired. The best defense is to populate your diet with high-fiber complex carbohydrates, combined with a little protein. This combination causes a slow release of blood sugar and thus keeps your energy levels sustained throughout the day. Choose natural energy foods such as fresh fruits over candy bars to maintain your energy levels.

Avoid high-fat meals and snacks too. They make you feel sluggish because fat is metabolized very slowly. Also, fatty foods increase fat droplets in your bloodstream. This reaction is de-energizing because it interferes with oxygen delivery to the brain and other tissues.

Make sure your diet is full of "antifatigue foods." These include iron-rich foods. Iron is a mineral that helps create hemoglobin, a protein in your red blood cells that carries oxygen from the lungs to the rest of your body. Oxygen is critical for converting foods to energy. Iron-rich foods include lean red meats, poultry, leafy green vegetables, and dried fruits.

Other antifatigue foods include those high in the B-complex vitamins, which are involved in nearly every reaction in the body, from the manufacture of new red blood cells to the metabolism of carbohydrates, fat, and protein. Whole grains, vegetables, and dairy products are good sources of B-complex vitamins.

As extra dietary insurance, supplement with an antioxidant formulation containing 100 percent of the daily values for vitamins and minerals. Vitamins and minerals are catalysts in many energy-producing reactions in the body.

HAVE YOU TRIED GRAZING THROUGHOUT THE DAY?

Take a tip from cows and other farm animals: Eat several small, healthy meals throughout the day. This practice helps maintain your blood-sugar levels, preventing fatigue. Frequent small meals also help prevent bingeing and are thus a good strategy if you're trying to lose body fat.

A good snack is one that combines a little protein with a complex carbohydrate. For example: fresh fruit and low-fat yogurt; rice cakes or high-fiber crackers with low-fat cheese; or a glass of skim milk and some raw veggies.

For a quick, convenient snack, try the protein/carbohydrate shakes or sports nutrition bars now available in grocery stores, pharmacies, and health food stores. These provide vitamins, minerals, and other nutrients and are a great way to get a nutritional lift during the day, especially at mid-morning and mid-afternoon.

HOW MUCH CAFFEINE DO YOU USE?

You know caffeine best as the ingredient in your coffee and tea that gets you going in the morning. Caffeine is the most widely used drug in the world, classified as a central nervous system stimulant. It can make your heart race. It gives you a wide-awake feeling, sometimes bordering on the jitters, depending on how much you take. Brewed coffee contains between 60 and 180 mg of caffeine; brewed tea, 25 to 100 mg; cola drinks, around 45 mg; and dark chocolate, between 5 and 35 mg. Caffeine is also found in over-the-counter diet pills because the drug speeds up the metabolic rate by as much as 16 percent.

While caffeine makes you feel peppy, it can exhaust you later. Too much caffeine stimulates the adrenal glands. The adrenals secrete adrenaline, a hormone that lets the body rapidly create energy in "fight or flight" situations. You feel an energy jolt as caffeine rushes throughout your body. But this energy jolt isn't what it seems. All that's happening is that caffeine strong-arms the body into emptying its energy reserves faster than it would normally. Once the effects of caffeine wear off—which occurs within about three and a half hours, on average—your energy dips, and you feel more tired than ever.

Too much caffeine can have unhealthy side effects, including nervousness, irritability, heart palpitations and arrhythmias, stomach upset, diarrhea, and frequent urination. Caffeine also causes moderate calcium loss. The amount of caffeine in one cup of coffee can up your calcium needs by 30 to 50 mg each day. This fact is important for women to know, since adequate daily calcium helps protect against osteoporosis. Caffeine also inhibits the absorption of the B-complex vitamin thiamin, important for carbohydrate metabolism, and can aggravate existing health problems, such as ulcers, heart disease, high blood pressure, and anemia.

It may be a good idea to moderate the amount of caffeine you take in each day, or avoid it altogether. If you do decide to quit coffee and tea, do so gradually. Withdrawal can cause painful headaches. You should talk to your doctor about how much coffee, tea, or other caffeinated beverages you drink, or whether you should cut them out.

TWO-MINUTE BLENDER BREAKFASTS

Each recipe makes one serving. Place all ingredients in a blender and blend until smooth.

1. Tofu Colada (290 calories)
1/2 cup silken tofu   1/2 cup skim milk
1/2 frozen banana   1 tablespoon honey
1/2 teaspoon coconut extract
1/2 cup crushed pineapple (canned in its own juice)

2. Peachy Protein Shake (370 calories)
8 oz. can of vanilla-flavored nutritional energy drink
1 cup frozen peaches   1/4 cup raw instant oatmeal

(With the addition of oatmeal, this shake makes a delicious, complete meal. You can purchase nutritional energy drinks at most pharmacies and supermarkets.)

3. Double Strawberry Freeze (270 calories)
1 cup skim milk   1 cup frozen strawberries
1 packet Strawberry Creme Carnation Instant Breakfast

4. Banana Soyshake (230 calories)
1/2 frozen banana   1 cup carob-flavored soy milk
1 tsp. instant coffee

5. Yogurt OrangeRas (215 calories)
1/2 plain non-fat yogurt   1/2 cup orange juice
1/2 cup frozen raspberries   1 tablespoon honey

6. Tropical Smoothie (355 calories)
1 cup orange peach mango juice
1 packet French Vanilla Carnation Instant Breakfast
3/4 cup papaya (bottled in light syrup—drain syrup and rinse papaya)
3–4 ice cubes, crushed

(You may substitute a frozen banana if papaya is not available.)

7. Double Chocolate Malt (365 calories)
1 cup skim milk   1/4 cup raw instant oatmeal
1 packet Classic Chocolate Malt Carnation Instant Breakfast
1 tablespoon fat-free chocolate syrup
3–4 ice cubes, crushed

ARE YOU WATERING YOUR BODY?

Water is a life-giving nutrient that makes up about 60 percent of your body weight. You can live up to 40 days without food, but you'll die within about six days without water.

If you feel thirsty, chances are you're already mildly dehydrated. Most people are dehydrated and don't know it. Dehydration can make you extremely tired, since water is involved in energy-producing processes in the body. Water also assists in nourishment by carrying nutrients to cells and transporting waste products away, as well as dissolving vitamins, minerals, proteins, glucose, and other nutrients so they can be used by the cells.

You can tell how well you've watered your body by checking the color of your urine. If it's clear, you're well-hydrated; if it's dark, you're not. Dark-colored urine indicates that metabolic wastes have accumulated without being adequately filtered from your system.

To get enough water, drink between eight to ten glasses (8 oz.) throughout the day. Instead of having a cup of coffee on your desk, substitute a water bottle or glass of water. Also, drink a glass or two before you exercise, sip water during exercise, and have another glass or two after exercise.

HAVE YOU BEEN TRYING TO EXERCISE REGULARLY?

As long as you're fueling yourself with the proper foods, exercise will recharge you, not sap your energy. Exercise makes your body more oxygen-efficient, so you use less oxygen in normal day-to-day activities. Regular exercise also reduces stress (a fatigue contributor) by naturally boosting mood-elevating brain chemicals that make you feel good. Be sure you're getting some physical activity (a minimum of 30 minutes) most days of the week.

HOW DO YOU START YOUR DAY?

The cause of much fatigue is psychological. A mentally draining day, an overbooked schedule, the pressures of the job—these are common stressors, and stress will wipe you out, physically and mentally. One way to prevent stress-producing fatigue is to start your day by quietly reading the Bible. Set aside some time for yourself in the morning—at least 10 to 20 minutes of solitude—when you can focus on God's Word.

God reveals to us in Psalm 1:1–3 the results of spending daily time reading the Bible: "Blessed is the man who does not walk in the counsel of the wicked or stand in the way of sinners or sit in the seat of mockers. But his delight is in the law of the LORD, and on his law he meditates day and night. He is like a tree planted by streams of water, which yields its fruit in season and whose leaf does not wither. Whatever he does prospers."

The life led separated from sin and secured to Scripture finds favor from God. Memorizing and reflecting on passages of Scripture is spiritually nourishing, productive, and renewing. It produces Christ-centered actions and attitudes that can help us better deal with the often stressful realities of life. Time alone with God has a calming effect that can ultimately boost your mental and physical energy.

LESSON OF THE DAY

Take actions daily that vitalize
rather than de-energize.

DAY 12

Exercise Booster Shots

No-Sweat Fitness Enhancers for Lifelong Health

Whether just starting a fitness program or renewing a commitment, everyone needs exercise booster shots from time to time to keep motivation from flagging. You're midway through this 21-day fitness program—how's your exercise motivation at this point? To keep it high, here are some practical tips:

READ TO SUCCEED

Reading articles and books on nutrition and exercise is an excellent inducement because it increases your knowledge of fitness and helps you maintain motivation. Don't neglect the Bible; it's the greatest self-help book of all, the source of truth on every aspect of life.

TWO-BY-TWO TRAINING

When I taught a women's bodyshaping course at the University of Southern Indiana, I observed that the women who were the most consistent in attendance were the ones who came to class with a friend or relative.

Research suggests the importance of support in sustaining motivation. Studies show that beginners are more successful when they work out with others, and people who exercise in groups have twice the adherence of those who go it alone. Researchers at the University of Georgia found that we're 80 percent more likely to stick to our exercise routine when it's done with a spouse or mate. Exercise partnerships are proving to be natural motivators. After all, you're less likely to duck out of an exercise appointment if your partner is counting on you to be there.

To make the most of partner training, here are some important tips:

- Choose exercise activities you both enjoy.
- Don't be competitive; be positive and encouraging.
- Your partner should be able to exercise at the same level you do.

DRESS FOR READINESS

Want to excuse-proof your workout plans for the day? Here's my favorite booster shot: When I get up in the morning, I don my exercise clothes (provided I have no business appointments) and wear them all day. That way, I'm ready for my workout. This keeps me thinking and feeling "exercise." I'm less likely to talk myself out of it if I'm already suited up.

PAY TO STAY

Owners of health clubs can tell plenty of stories about members who paid for memberships but never reappeared after the first month. So it's hard to say whether plunking down money for a fitness program will help you stick to it. But for some people, it may. In one study, exercisers committed to participating in a six-month aerobics program by paying $40—which was reimbursable if they stuck with the program each week. Anyone who failed to work out weekly would lose the deposit. There was a control group who exercised but wasn't required to place the $40 deposit. Interestingly, the group who made the deposit had the best stick-to-it-iveness—97 percent, compared with the control group whose adherence was only 19 percent.

Maybe you've been exercising on your own so far. If your motivation's dipping, consider signing up for a class or paying for a membership at a health club.

THE FAMILY THAT GETS FIT TOGETHER STAYS FIT

Family commitments can often get in the way of a consistent fitness program. Statistics bear this out: According to the Centers for Disease Control and Prevention, 56 percent of men and 46 percent of women between the ages of 18 and 29 exercise regularly, but those percentages fall to 44 percent and 40 percent, respectively, among people 30 to 44—probably due to shifting fitness patterns after marriage and children. Let's face it: When you have kids, it's harder and harder to find time for exercise.

Children are becoming heavier and unhealthier too. According to one national report, since 1980 there has been a 6 percent increase in childhood obesity rates, with 21 percent of teenagers now considered significantly overweight. What makes this increase so troubling is that unhealthy weight in children is related to many of the same chronic disease risk factors as unhealthy weight in adults. That's a scary thought—but fortunately you have some control over your children's health.

Children learn primarily by example. If your eating and exercise habits are poor, your children's probably will be too. Yet if your children see that you value exercise and enjoy it, they are likely to do the same. A 1990 study found that children of active mothers were twice as likely to be active as those with non-exercising mothers; children of active fathers were three-and-one-half times as likely to be active. And when both parents worked out, their kids were nearly six times as likely to be active. Your influence is a powerful tool God has given you to use in caring for your children.

Why not start exercising as a family? It may not be as hard as you think. Consider:

- Invest in a special jogging stroller.
- Try biking, hiking, swimming, or skating as a family.
- Many health clubs, YMCAs, community recreation centers, and churches offer fitness programs for youngsters.
- Play with your kids regularly in vigorous outdoor games.

TUNE OUT TO TUNE UP

Psychologists working with athletes and exercisers have found that if you concentrate on something outside yourself while exercising (technically called "external focus") rather than on what you're doing, you're more likely to persevere—and you'll do your best work.

In one interesting study reported in *Psychology Today*, ten college students in a physical education class were divided into two experimental groups. The first group was told to concentrate on how their leg muscles felt and how their heart rate increased while exercising on stationary bikes for thirty minutes. The second group, the external-focus group, filled out a questionnaire on body image while pedaling. The first group, who had focused on their bodies, felt their exercise session took longer. Even though they perceived they had exercised harder, they had not. The researchers concluded that external focus works better because it makes us less aware of fatigue and discomfort, and thus it's easier to keep up the activity.

To shore up your stick-to-it-iveness, why not try external focus while you're exercising? Here are some ideas:

- Memorize Scripture passages.
- Listen to sermon tapes.
- Listen to your favorite music.
- Focus on the lyrics of the music in exercise class or sing along quietly.
- Don't focus on the time. Cover the timer with a towel.
- Watch television or read a magazine or a good book.
- "Pray continually" (1 Thess. 5:17).

MENTAL WARM-UP

Finally, take a lesson from competitive athletes: Start thinking about the benefits of your upcoming workout. The calories you'll burn. The muscle you'll firm. The stress-relieving chemicals that will flood your system. Imagine how invigorated you'll feel afterward. Replay this information in your head. Now go for it—you'll be amazed at what you can accomplish today.

LESSON OF THE DAY

Don't get stuck in an exercise rut. There are plenty of ways to give yourself exercise booster shots from time to time.

DAY 13

Turn the Tables on Temptation

The Best Weapons to Stop Overeating Now

Temptation can be the downfall of even the most well-intentioned fitness efforts. Giving in to temptation too often can become a bad habit, and before long you've retreated to a pattern of unhealthy living. If you want to turn the tables on temptation, here are six Bible-based strategies you can employ.

1. Pray

In the Lord's Prayer (Matt. 6:9–13), in which Jesus teaches his disciples how to pray, he says, "Lead us not into temptation, but deliver us from the evil one." Jesus acknowledges that we're easily led astray and that we need God to keep us on the straight and narrow. By ourselves, we're powerless to resist temptation. That's why we need to depend completely on God for strength. The more you depend on God to see you through temptation, the greater your ability to overcome it.

When tempted, pray for help. You may even want to use the Lord's Prayer.

2. Prioritize

God once told the Israelites: "Give careful thought to your ways. You have planted much, but have harvested little. You eat, but never have enough. You drink, but never have your fill. You put on clothes, but are not warm. You earn wages, only to put them in a purse with holes in it" (Hag. 1:5–6).

Whatever the people did, flopped big-time. Does that sound a little like your last fitness effort? You tried hard to get in shape, but with few results. You made a stab at eating right but fell prey to temptation at every turn. Why?

Because you may have ignored something that's vital to whatever you undertake in life: your relationship with God. Unless you put God first in your life, everything you try to do—including getting in shape—will be to little avail. Take a God-first, not self-first, attitude. The more you are in concert with God's will for your life, the easier it will be to resist temptation, because your desire will be to honor and praise him in all things.

3. Publicize

Let a few key loving, caring, and trustworthy people know that you are trying to change your lifestyle and need their help in avoiding temptation. You can better resist food temptations by bringing your situation out into the open and enlisting the understanding and support of others.

If you keep your struggles bottled up, you're destined for disaster. Secret struggles over food, or whatever, can turn into obsessions. Opening up to other people, and to God, can release you from the grip of temptation and keep you on the right track.

4. Plug into Scripture

When Jesus was tempted in the desert three times by the devil (Matt. 4:1–11), he quoted Scripture each time to counter the attack. After Jesus had resisted Satan's temptations, "the devil left him." What an encouragement to know you can repel temptations with Scripture. Have a bank of memorized passages to plug into.

Second Corinthians 10:5 says: "We take captive every thought to make it obedient to Christ." This piece of scriptural advice is really a form of "thought-stopping," a practical way to keep yourself from obsessively dwelling on counterproductive thoughts. When those thoughts creep in, simply yell "Stop!" (in your mind), and you'll be amazed at how well you can get them under control.

Here's how thought-stopping can work in the light of Scripture: Suppose you get the urge to eat a few pints of ice cream. To bring that urge under control, stop yourself and ask whether gorging on ice cream is an act of obedience to God. You know it isn't, since God's will for you is to make healthy choices. Then see if you still want to go ahead with your binge.

Scripture is the "light" of understanding. Plug into it for correction and direction whenever you're in the dark.

5. Permit Yourself Favorite Foods

In a world filled with delicious but unhealthy things to eat and drink, you are bound to be tempted often. Temptation loses its power over you when you give yourself permission to indulge in certain foods periodically without bingeing on them.

No foods should be off-limits forever. You'll only obsess about them and eventually resort to bingeing. Instead, plan to eat a treat on a certain day, at a certain time—without eating on impulse. Impulsive eating leads to more impulsive eating, not to mention a pile of guilt. When you plan in this manner, you give yourself permission to eat, and there is no guilt.

6. Part Company with Temptation

Sometimes when you're tempted, you just have to remove yourself physically from the temptation, or vice versa: "Flee the evil desires of youth, and pursue righteousness, faith, love and peace, along with those who call on the Lord out of a pure heart" (2 Tim. 2:22). In other words: Run away from temptation.

Avoid the restaurant that serves only fried foods. Stop buying fattening foods, and stock your cupboards with healthy foods instead. To keep yourself from overindulging at parties, eat a healthy, filling meal before you go. Don't frequent bakeries, or bake cookies and brownies. The list of ways to physically avoid temptations is endless. Think about what your food temptations are and how you can circumvent them. Always keep in mind: God gives you the strength to resist unhealthy longings.

There's Always a Way Out

With every temptation, God provides an escape route: "No temptation has seized you except what is common to man. And God is faithful; he will not let you be tempted beyond what you can bear. But when you are tempted, he will also provide a way out so you can stand up under it" (1 Cor. 10:13).

It is encouraging to know you're not alone in temptation; everyone struggles with it. Even more encouraging is knowing you can trust God to help you resist it. Every time you're tempted, he has already provided a way out. And it could be any number of avenues, including prayer, Scripture, renewed strength, help from other believers, or a solution that miraculously presents itself. Don't ignore the escape routes God has already mapped out for you.

LESSON OF THE DAY

No matter how strong the temptation, God has already mapped out your escape route.

DAY 14

From Here to Serenity

Spiritual Secrets of Emotional Fitness

Negative emotions can cause people to self-medicate with junk food, alcohol, or drugs. Although these things may temporarily make you feel better, they're potentially destructive in the long run. As you take this journey toward better fitness, it's important to understand how negative emotions can affect health, and what to do about them.

EMOTIONS AND YOUR HEALTH

Medical experts estimate that envy, hatred, guilt, repressed anger, and other stress-producing emotions may account for more than 60 percent of all illnesses, particularly heart disease, stroke, and cancer.

In a recent study, 1,305 healthy men between the ages of 40 and 90 were tested on their ability to control anger, then followed for 7 years to see who suffered heart attacks. The findings: The men with the shortest fuse had more than triple the risk of nonfatal heart attacks and fatal coronary heart disease, even after the researchers adjusted for smoking and alcohol use.

Many studies in the last 20 years have found that people who harbor hostile emotions have a much higher rate of heart disease and its warning signs than do people who are not so hostile. Other studies have found that men who are self-involved tend to have more extensively blocked arteries (a heart attack risk) than men who are less self-involved. Self-centered heart patients are also more prone to second heart attacks. Scientists theorize that frequent surges in stress-related chemicals contribute to heart-damaging processes.

Anxiety causes physical damage too. Researchers from Ohio State University investigated the effects of exam stress on students. Their experiment revealed that stress interfered with the function of "natural killer cells," which help the body combat foreign invaders that cause disease. The stress brought on by exams also reduced the body's production of interferon, a type of protein that fights viruses and boosts immunity.

STRESS MANAGEMENT FROM ABOVE

Although the connection between emotions and health is not fully understood, the ability to handle emotions constructively, which is part of stress management, is considered an essential component of a healthy lifestyle. The good news is that God has a stress management program for your life—one that will move you from stress to serenity. You'll be less likely to indulge in unhealthy behaviors, and thus you'll move closer to better physical health. Today, consider the following dos and don'ts and how you can use them to manage stress.

DON'T:

Fret

Are you a worrywart—you know, always turning everything into a worst-case scenario? Chronic worry is a draining, immobilizing emotion. You obsess over things that may or may not happen in the future. As Mark Twain once said, "I have known a great many troubles, but most of them never happened."

The best antidote to worry is found in Paul's message to the Philippians: "Do not be anxious about anything, but in everything, by prayer and petition, with thanksgiving, present your requests to God. And the peace of God, which transcends all understanding, will guard your hearts and minds in Christ Jesus" (Phil. 4:6–7).

Worry keeps you from focusing on the present, and worse, it takes your focus off God. Paul's solution? Replace worry with prayer. And with gratitude, put everything into God's care. The result is a God-given peace that guards your morality and thought life—in other words, keeps you from sinning and from needless emotional distress.

Fume

Anger is probably the strongest of all emotions—with positive and negative results. On the positive side, anger may move us to fight an injustice, as Jesus did when he cleared the temple of moneychangers, or to protect our family. Anger can be very useful by prompting us to action. On the negative side, anger—especially when repressed or unresolved—can be dangerous, leading to sinful behavior, violence, and crime. Scripture advises, "Refrain from anger and turn from wrath; do not fret—it leads only to evil" (Ps. 37:8).

The anger described here is rage; "wrath" can be translated as "poison." Thus, the passage is talking about a dangerous anger, one that can eat away at you if not controlled. We are to break free from this anger. If we don't, it can fester and poison our relationships, destroy our health, and ultimately block the way to godly living. How do you abandon anger? By giving it to God. "Turn from" in the Hebrew means to forsake, or leave in someone else's control. If you suffer from a festering anger, the solution is to turn it over to God and trust him to restore your serenity.

DO:

Forgive Others

People do things to us, and we to them. We lie to, cheat on, abuse, betray, and hurt each other, and more. These things are a sad, unfortunate fact of life. After being hurt, we can carry the pain in our hearts or let it go. Holding the pain in, many medical experts theorize, inhibits the immune system and leaves us vulnerable to life-threatening illnesses such as heart disease and cancer. An unforgiving spirit can be physically destructive.

An unforgiving spirit is also spiritually destructive. In Matthew 18:21–35, Jesus tells the story of a king who cancelled the entire debt of a servant who owed him a large sum of money. The servant had a fellow servant who owed him a small amount. Rather than cancel the debt, the servant had him thrown into prison when he couldn't pay. Enraged, the king turned the unforgiving servant over to jailors until he could repay his debt. Jesus ends the parable by saying, "This is how my heavenly Father will treat each of you unless you forgive your brother from your heart."

The message is clear. God is the King, and we are his servants, carrying a debt of sin we can't pay. In his death on the cross, Christ paid our debts in full and God forgave our sins. Because of God's forgiveness, we are to demonstrate the same forgiving spirit toward others. If we don't, there's a spiritual penalty to pay. We'll be corrected by suffering on earth and judged in heaven for violating Christ's law of forgiveness. Although it's often difficult to forgive, it's a requirement for Christian living.

Focus on Others

One of the best stress management techniques you can employ is servanthood. Do something for somebody else— serve meals at a soup kitchen, sign up for a ministry, go on a mission trip. Pick a cause you want to support and volunteer your time and talents to help make a difference. You won't be sorry, and you'll be better off, physically and spiritually.

Research shows you can experience the same physiological changes when you help others as you do when you exercise. Heart rate and breathing decrease, and feel-good endorphins are released—all of which power up the immune system. In a landmark study of volunteerism, researchers found that those who helped regularly were physically healthier than people who volunteered only once a year. The regular helpers reported fewer illnesses from colds, allergies, and asthma; less depression; fewer aches and pains; and a sense of calmness and well-being. In another fascinating study, investigators at the University of Michigan followed 2,700 people for more than a decade to see how volunteerism affected their health and found that volunteering was linked to a lower death rate.

Jesus demonstrated servanthood by wrapping a towel around his waist as a lowly servant would do and washing his disciples' feet. If Christ is willing to serve, so must we—in ways that bring honor to God.

Feed Yourself Spiritually

We need constant spiritual nourishment, just as we need physical food. God once commanded the prophet Ezekiel to eat a scroll containing his message. Ezekiel did so, and "it tasted as sweet as honey" in his mouth (Ezek. 3:1–3). Figuratively, we too must internalize the messages of the Bible by memorizing passages of Scripture and making them part of us. Wonderful things can happen when we do. As Proverbs 4:20–22 reminds us: "My son, pay attention to what I say; listen closely to my words. Do not let them out of your sight, keep them within your heart; for they are life to those who find them and health to a man's whole body."

For those who heed it, study it, and internalize it, Scripture energizes and enlivens. The next time you're stressed out, reach for the Bible. It's the best tranquilizer around, and the effects won't wear off.

LESSON OF THE DAY

Negative emotions can harm;
total devotion can heal.

DAY 15

Eat Out and Still Eat Right

A SWAT Team of Tips to Defend You Against Overeating in Restaurants

Where's it easier to stick to a healthy diet—at home or in a restaurant? Home, says a recent study.

Researchers from the University of North Carolina report that women (ages 19 to 50) who eat their meals at home have the best eating habits and get a balanced intake of important nutrients. The worst eaters are younger women who eat a third of their meals at fast-food restaurants.

Uh-oh. If you're like most people I know, you eat out often. After all, it's easier and faster. According to the National Restaurant Association, Americans eat out 4.1 times a week. Many of those meals are eaten at fast-food restaurants, where food is typically high in fat and sodium. The NPD group, a customer research firm that tracks American eating habits annually, said that during a two-week period in 1996, we swilled 15,000 more sodas, gobbled up 8,000 more orders of fries, wolfed down 6,000 more hamburgers, and feasted on 5,000 more chicken bits than we did during a similar period in 1995.

But does dining out have to spell dieting disaster? Not necessarily. These days, healthy foods are served practically everywhere—even in vending machines.

You don't have to be a recluse while sprucing up your health habits. You're free to go out to restaurants, even fast-food places, to enjoy breakfast, lunch, or dinner with your friends, family, or business associates. Nor should you pass up invitations to parties or other social events just because you're on a healthy eating program.

What follows are some practical guidelines for making healthy choices at any type of restaurant, as well as for enjoying parties and other events.

RESTAURANTS FOR BREAKFAST

- Order scrambled egg whites, or scrambled egg substitutes (such as EggBeaters). Request that the eggs be cooked without added oil.
- For carbohydrates, your best bets are grits, oatmeal, cream of wheat, oat bran, or other whole grain cereal with skim milk. Other good choices include English muffins or whole-wheat toast (avoid sweet rolls and buns).
- Fresh fruits and juices are excellent choices to round out your breakfast.

ASIAN RESTAURANTS

- Select entrees made with lean proteins (such as chicken and fish) and vegetables. Some good suggestions for ordering are Moo Goo Gai Pan, Szechuan Shrimp or Chicken, and sushi.

- Request that the sauce be served on the side, or forgo it altogether.
- Order steamed rice.
- Asian restaurants serve generous helpings. Consider ordering one entree and splitting it with a friend, unless you want to take the leftovers home.

ITALIAN RESTAURANTS

- For an appetizer, try vegetable antipasto (if available), with dressing on the side.
- Look for entrees such as grilled chicken and fish as well as Italian dishes that are marked as low in fat.
- Avoid entrees prepared in cream sauce or Alfredo sauce.
- If you're really being strict, ask the waiter to leave the rolls and breadsticks in the kitchen.
- When ordering a dinner salad, ask for dressing on the side.
- Opt for vegetables as your side dish over pasta. Make sure the vegetables are steamed.

MEXICAN RESTAURANTS

- Rather than be tempted by fat-laden tortilla chips, ask your server to substitute corn tortillas, or plain baked tortillas, to dip.
- Good choices are grilled foods—such as fajitas, mesquite-grilled chicken or fish—or baked entrees. If ordering fajitas, request that the chicken and vegetables be grilled dry.
- Grilled chicken, shrimp, or lean meat entrees are good choices.
- Request pico de gallo (a mixture of chopped tomatoes, green peppers, and onions) instead of salsa. Guacamole is a next-best choice. Made with avocado, it's a little high in fat, but the fat is healthy, natural vegetable fat.

- Mexican rice or black bean soup are nice accompaniments to a Mexican meal. So are the refried beans, but check first to see whether they are prepared in lard, or baked or boiled, and seasoned. If they aren't refried in lard, enjoy them.
- A dinner salad with nonfat salad dressing is a healthy meal-starter.

STEAKHOUSE

- Avoid creamed soups; stick to clear, broth-type soups.
- Order grilled lean meat, chicken, salmon, or other fish (prepared without oil).
- For a side dish, select a steamed vegetable such as broccoli, a baked potato or sweet potato, or steamed rice.
- At the salad bar, stick to fresh vegetables and nonfat or low-fat salad dressing. Many salad bars serve fresh fruit too—load up on it and put it aside for dessert.

HOMESTYLE OR CAFETERIA RESTAURANT

- Request grilled or lemon chicken, turkey breast without the gravy, or white fish prepared without sauce or oil.
- Order steamed rice, a dry baked potato, or corn prepared without oil or fat.
- Select steamed vegetables (no sauce or butter), salad with nonfat dressing, or carrot/vegetable medley prepared without butter or margarine.
- Blindfold yourself when passing by the dessert line.

DELI

- A good protein choice is sliced turkey or chicken breast.
- Request that your sandwich be prepared on whole-grain bread.

- Order steamed vegetable side dishes, if available, or a plain salad with non-fat dressing.
- Request that your sandwich be prepared with mustard only—no mayonnaise or butter.

PIZZERIA

- Pizza is not unhealthy, as long you don't eat it every night. The crust is high in carbohydrates, the tomato sauce is generally fat-free, and the cheese is usually made from part-skim milk mozzarella. But watch out for the toppings—they can be loaded with fat.
- Order an all-vegetable pizza and ask the cook to lighten up on the cheese.
- There's no rule that says you have to order pizza at a pizza place. Have a salad instead.

FAST-FOOD RESTAURANTS

- Your best bets for breakfast are cereals (if available), skim or low-fat milk, muffins, and fruit juice.
- The best sandwich choices are grilled or broiled chicken (no sauce or mayonnaise), pitas, or any sandwich advertised as "lite" or lower in fat.
- Most fast-food establishments have salads on their menus; grilled chicken salads are your best bets. Order fat-free salad dressing with your salad. If there's a salad bar, stick to fresh vegetables and fat-free salad dressing.
- At fast-food restaurants that serve fish, order baked fish, rice, or baked potato, vegetables, and salad.
- Other good fast-food choices include plain baked potatoes and chili.
- For dessert, look for low-fat soft-serve frozen yogurt.

VENDING MACHINE CHOICES

- Popcorn (non-buttered or "lite").
- Low-fat pretzels.
- Granola bars.
- Tomato juice.
- Fresh fruit.
- Non-oiled nuts.
- Nonfat fig bars.
- Whole-wheat crackers.

ENTERTAINMENT/SPORTING EVENTS

- Popcorn is a healthy choice, if it's air-popped and not drenched with butter.
- Baked pretzels make a healthy snack.
- Pack a sports nutrition bar for the movies, instead of indulging in movie candy.
- Low-fat soft-serve frozen yogurt is a good choice.

PARTIES

- Eat a meal before you go to the party, to fend off hunger pangs and cravings.
- Snack on fresh vegetables and fruit (but pass up the dip), popcorn (if it's air-popped), or baked tortilla corn chips (just a few).
- Instead of a cocktail, drink a diet soda or carbonated water with a twist of lemon or lime.

TRAVEL

- Pack sports nutrition bars, high-fiber crackers or rice cakes, cut-up fresh vegetables, fresh fruits, or cans of water-packed tuna to eat on the road or while in flight.

- In airports, look for popcorn (air-popped, of course), or low-fat soft-serve frozen yogurt as snack foods.

On the surface, it may not seem like fun to limit yourself to certain foods when eating out. But rest assured: The ability to make healthy choices at restaurants is just one more positive step toward banishing bad eating habits. You'll feel better, and your body will love you for it.

LESSON OF THE DAY

Every healthy choice you make—even at restaurants—moves you closer to wholeness.

Don't Pull Your Food Triggers

How to Tame Your Eating Urges

I was so bored, I ate a whole bag of chips" . . . "My husband and I had a fight. Afterward, I headed straight for the refrigerator" . . . "I eat really healthy at home, but whenever I'm at my in-laws', I go hog-wild."

Can you relate to these situations? Are you likely to eat for all the wrong reasons? Many of us have experienced the feeling of being out of control over food—and the guilt that comes later. The solution is to identify what triggers out-of-control eating, then create strategies to curb the urge.

Today, you'll "ID" your food triggers and figure out ways to prevent unhealthy overeating. But first, let's explore some of the reasons we tend to overeat. Many have less to do with hunger, and more to do with people, places, and pressures.

PEOPLE

The power of people, particularly groups, to influence our behavior is more common and subtle than you might imagine. In a group, we want to "fit in," so we try to conform to the group behavior. A group can be a work group, a circle of friends, a small group Bible study, a family. Groups can influence us positively or negatively. Since many group activities center around eating and drinking, you have to be on your guard to not fall in with unhealthy group behaviors. Even Scripture warns: "Do not be with heavy drinkers of wine, or with gluttonous eaters of meat" (Prov. 23:20 NASB). As you pursue better health and fitness, there are two kinds of people to avoid—those who eat too much and those who drink too much. Both are bad influences if you desire a beneficial lifestyle.

If people tend to trigger unhealthy habits in your life, here are some strategies to consider:

- If you're going to dinner with a group of friends and are concerned that you'll overeat, eat some natural high-fiber foods (such as raw vegetables or fruit) before you go. You'll be less likely to pig out later.
- Have a good, hard exercise session the day of the gathering with your family or friends. On workout days you're less likely to undo the beneficial effects of exercise by deciding to splurge.
- Offer to bring a couple of your own dishes (low-fat, of course) to the gathering.
- Try to arrange activities with these people that don't include food, such as going to the movies, a concert, or play.
- Cultivate a circle of supportive friends who also practice healthy lifestyles.
- To reiterate: Be a fitness witness. You may be in the minority in a certain group, but you have power to sway the majority. Researchers who have studied the minority influence in mock jury deliberations have found that a dissenting minority was most influential when it took a consistent position in a confident manner. By sticking to

your values and healthy habits, you can have a positive impact on the lifestyles of your family and friends.

PLACES

Locales, certain rooms in our homes, our cars—these can all be triggers associated with eating. Some strategies:

- If driving home from work takes you by your favorite drive-through, find another route.
- Do you overeat or over-snack in front of the television? If so, make it a rule in your house to always eat in the dining room.
- If you're vulnerable to over-snacking the moment you walk in the door after work, revamp your daily diet so that you're less ravenous. Make sure to eat a healthy snack at mid-morning and mid-afternoon, and don't skip lunch. Or instead of raiding the fridge after coming home, head to the gym.
- Like to nibble in the kitchen while fixing dinner? Those extra bites can really mount up, calorie-wise. Chew some sugarless gum, sip water or diet soda, or keep low-calorie snacks such as raw veggies on hand while you're cooking. If you don't have time to cut up vegetables, buy pre-cut veggies (or fruits) from the grocery store, or take advantage of the store's salad bar, which usually has plenty of freshly cut items.

Late-night snacking on high-fat or high-sugar goodies can be a problem too. It is particularly defeating, since fewer calories are burned when you're sleeping. Much of your late-night snack can end up being stored as fat. If late-night eating is your downfall, don't try to stop cold turkey. Simply substitute healthier munchies: non-fat yogurt (very filling and acts as a natural sleep aid), a low-calorie dessert, fresh fruit, or raw veggies.

PRESSURES

Pressures in life can boil over into emotions, which are among the biggest reasons we overeat. Some of the common pressure-triggers include: boredom, loneliness, anger, anxiety, and depression. Stressed out, we eat to soothe our troubles rather than to curb the natural sensation of hunger. Positive emotions can trigger binges too. Whatever the source, you need to ask yourself if you're eating because you're hungry or because your emotions are running high. Also, review Day 14 for strategies on dealing with stress.

An occasional indulgence is harmless, unless it turns into repeated bingeing. Then you've got cause for alarm. Here are some suggestions to keep you from pulling the pressure-trigger:

- If you're prone to emotional eating, clear the kitchen cabinets of binge food.
- If you can't eat just one handful of chips, don't buy large bags. Purchase single servings instead, or don't buy chips at all. Or if your favorite indulgence is chocolate, keep it out of the house. Instead, go to an expensive candy store on occasion and buy just a single serving of chocolate.
- Eat a variety of foods in moderation; this will put a lid on your desire to overeat. Fill up on high-fiber foods too. They take up a lot of space in your stomach, so you're less likely to gorge on them.
- Exercise relieves anxiety and depression; it's the perfect antidote to emotional eating because it helps dissipate the emotions that cause it.
- Distract yourself with a non-food-related activity, like exercising, reading, pursuing a favorite hobby, listening to music, writing letters, surfing the Internet (one of the best distractions yet), or soaking in a hot bath.

- Make a list of twenty-five things to do other than eat. Keep your list handy.
- Typical "comfort foods" such as chocolate, ice cream, milk and cookies, or chips tend to be laced with sugar, fat, and salt. While they may temporarily deflate your emotions, they ultimately inflate your waistline. The good news is that not all comfort foods are bad for you. There are plenty of healthy good-mood foods to choose from. Whole grains, for example, contain an amino acid that helps boost a mood-elevating brain chemical. Lean proteins such as chicken, tuna, and turkey have another type of amino acid that elevates brain chemicals involved in boosting energy and helping the body better cope with stress. In short, a healthy diet, rich with natural foods, can positively affect your behavior and energy levels.

To follow a healthy diet more consistently, it's first necessary to identify the people-places-pressures that trigger your loss of control over food. Then, with the help of today's lesson, strategize how to gain mastery over them. Here's a worksheet to help you map out appropriate strategies.

My Personal Food Triggers   **My Strategies for Mastery**

People: *Strategy:*

_____   _____
_____   _____
_____   _____

Places: *Strategy:*

_____   _____
_____   _____
_____   _____

Pressures: *Strategy:*

_____   _____
_____   _____
_____   _____

LESSON OF THE DAY

Lesson of the Day: People, places, and pressures trigger overeating. By identifying your personal food triggers, you can strategize to immunize yourself against unhealthy longings.

Toward a New Food Attitude

End Problem Eating in a Flash

Our dieting-crazed society has attached meanings to food that were never meant to be. As a result, you can get locked in a lifelong struggle with what you think are the forces of good foods and evil foods. Eating becomes a test of moral character. You're a "bad" or "weak" person if you eat a food that's not on your diet.

That's irrational thinking. What you eat, or don't eat, certainly doesn't determine your character. If you tend to view food as good or bad, you must change that attitude or stay hopelessly chained to unhealthy feelings over food.

Today, I want you to internalize one simple truth that has the power to change your food attitude instantly. It can help you stop restrictive, bound-to-fail dieting. It can let you enjoy food and eat delicious meals. And, it can even let you indulge in desserts from time to time—without feeling guilty.

For starters, food is not your enemy. Food is not to be feared or demonized as "bad." The simple truth is this: Food is a gift from God. You can see this throughout Scripture, beginning in the first book of the Bible when God gave Adam and Eve the gift of fruits and vegetables: "I give you every seed-bearing plant on the face of the whole earth and every tree that has fruit with seed in it. They will be yours for food" (Gen. 1:29).

After the Flood, God enlarged the gift. When Noah and his family emerged from the ark, God told them they could eat meat: "Everything that lives and moves will be food for you. Just as I gave you the green plants, I now give you everything" (Gen. 9:3).[1]

When we pray, "Give us today our daily bread" (Matt. 6:11), we acknowledge that food is indeed a gift from God and not something we make on our own. And God gives us important guidelines as to how to handle his gift of food. For example:

SELECT FOODS WISELY

While no food is bad, there are many foods known to be more "nutrient-dense" than others. Nutrient-dense foods are those that provide multiple nutrients but aren't too high in calories. Fruits, vegetables, whole grains, lean proteins, and low-fat dairy products are examples of nutrient-dense foods. They pack many health-building nutrients in every bite. By contrast, foods like potato chips, soft drinks, and pastries provide plenty of calories but few nutrients. Most (but not all) of your food choices should come from nutrient-dense foods for optimum health.

MODERATE YOUR INTAKE

Eating fried chicken every night or huge helpings of dessert after every dinner is a form of gluttony—the lack of restraint in eating and drinking. Proverbs 23:21 says that "drunkards and gluttons become poor"; in other words, overindulgence in food and drink leads to all forms of ruin, from physical to spiritual. Gorging on food, or abusing alcohol, can be signs of a spiritual problem. *You're self-medicating with food and alcohol instead of turning to God for solace and solutions.* And there's no question that food and alcohol abuse is health-destructive. Among other problems, food abuse leads to obesity. And alcohol abuse has a harmful effect on every organ in the body, particularly the heart, liver, and brain.

God created us with two signals that tell us when to eat and how much to eat. The "when" is hunger; the "how much" is satiety (the natural feeling of fullness). They work in balance. About every four hours, the body sends hunger signals—in the form of hunger pangs, weakness, or loss of attention span. Eating a meal relieves these feelings. About twenty minutes into the meal, the body sends satiety signals. You feel full and don't want to eat anymore. If you gulp down your food in less than twenty minutes, you're likely to keep eating because your satiety signal hasn't been sent. Stretching your meal out for at least twenty minutes helps you eat just the right amount. If you eat when you're hungry and stop when you're full, you'll have an easier time keeping your weight in check.

THINK OF FOOD AS PHYSICAL NOURISHMENT

The most basic and essential function of food is to provide nutrients needed for life and health. The very structures of your body, the fuel that powers your cells, and the body processes that keep you going—these ultimately come from and rely on food.

A biblical illustration of how food strengthens and nourishes is found in 1 Samuel 14:24–29. King Saul, on impulse, had forbidden his army under oath to eat anything until evening, after the battle was over. He put a curse on any soldier who would dare disobey the edict. None of the troops ate any food, and they became fatigued. Unaware of his father's order, Jonathan found some honey in the woods and ate it. The moment he tasted it, "his eyes brightened" (v. 27). When you're hungry and under-nourished, there are physical signs. You look pale and tired, often with dark circles under your eyes. But as it did with Jonathan, eating invigorates and revitalizes, and your whole appearance changes for the better.

Once you begin to look at the divine gift of food as a source of physical nourishment, it will be your servant, not your master. You'll learn to eat for nourishment and energy, not for self-medication.

ENJOY YOUR MEALS

On their missionary trip to Lystra, Paul and Barnabas began witnessing to the crowd about God and the evidence of his existence, in nature and in his provision for humanity: "He has shown kindness by giving you rain from heaven and crops in their seasons; he provides you with plenty of food and fills your hearts with joy" (Acts 14:17). What this passage reveals is that in providing physical nourishment, God also grants us a satisfying gladness that comes from the enjoyment of food. He wants us to enjoy food, not go on guilt trips over it.

RECEIVE FOOD WITH THANKSGIVING

When you get a gift, it's customary to thank the giver—which is why we say grace at meals. Moses set the example for this when he told the Israelites: "When you have eaten and are satisfied, praise the Lord your God for the good land he has given you" (Deut. 8:10). In the New Testament, we see Jesus continuing the tradition. In his miracle of feeding the 5,000, Jesus thanked God before distributing the food to the crowd (John 6:11). At the Last Supper, he gave thanks before giving the wine and bread to his disciples (Luke 22:17–19). Follow our Lord's example: Give thanks at meals. Table prayers represent yet another opportunity to thank God for his care and provision.

Once you accept that food is a gift from God, you'll begin a healthier relationship with it. You'll select your food more wisely, appreciate it as physical nourishment, enjoy it in moderation, and thank God for this precious, life-giving gift.

LESSON OF THE DAY

Food is a divine gift to be enjoyed in moderation and received with thanksgiving for its life-giving, health-sustaining nourishment.

DAY 18

Handle Your Health with Prayer

The Most Powerful Prescription in the World

Prayer is a conversation with God, confessing our sins, thanking him for his blessings, and making requests according to his will. The wonderful privilege of prayer places us in God's very presence so he can work in our lives. Today, we'll look at the relationship between prayer and health and at how God's direct intervention, or the comfort of his presence, can positively affect our well-being.

PRAYER AND MEDICAL CARE

Lately, prayer has been in the spotlight—as a factor in health and healing in medicine. Research shows that prayer can accelerate and improve the healing process. One of the most famous examples of this involved 393 patients who were admitted to a coronary care unit at San Francisco General Hospital for medical treatment in 1988. Half the patients were prayed for by a group of Christians, yet were unaware of the prayers on their behalf; the other half (the control group) were not prayed for.

What followed was quite remarkable. The first group healed much better and required fewer medical interventions than the control group. By contrast, the control group needed more assistance from ventilators, more antibiotics, and more diuretics than the other group. The researchers who conducted this study felt that Christian prayer was therapeutic to heart patients. *Prayer is so powerful that it can even help people who are unaware they are being prayed for.*

But we don't need research to prove that prayer works. The Bible does that for us.

BIBLICAL ACCOUNTS OF PRAYER AND HEALING

When we're sick, before running to the medicine chest or doctor's office, we need to involve God right away through prayer— through our prayers and the prayers of others. God uses these prayers in mighty ways. In Acts 28:7–8, a man on the island of Malta was suffering from fever and dysentery. Scripture says, "Paul went in to see him and, after prayer, placed his hands on him and healed him." The man was cured, but not until after Paul prayed. The healing on Malta suggests that prayer is a must-do first step in restoration.

There are two narratives in Scripture that by their contrast teach volumes about the importance of asking God to intervene in our lives when we are ill. The first is the story of King Hezekiah, told in 2 Kings 20:1–7. The king is on his deathbed, and the prophet Isaiah tells him, "This is what the Lord says: Put your house in order, because you are going to die; you will not recover."

Hezekiah, a man of devout faith, prays earnestly to God for recovery: "Remember, O Lord, how I have walked before you faithfully and with wholehearted devotion and have done what is good in your eyes."

What does God do in response? Even before Isaiah is out the door, God answers Hezekiah's prayer: "I have heard your prayer and seen your tears; I will heal you." Not only that, he promises to extend the king's life by fifteen years. Then, through Isaiah, God prescribes a medicinal cure that leads to recovery—an act that demonstrates how prayer and medication can effectively work together.

This remarkable narrative reveals two important aspects about the nature of God. First, he is a personal God, capable of experiencing great emotion. The very fact that *he sees Hezekiah's tears* reveals as much. Think of how you feel when you see others cry out of grief. Don't their tears flood your emotions with compassion, empathy, and love? So it is with God, but even more so. God is more compassionate, more empathetic, and more loving than we can fathom. He can be closer to us than even our closest friend.

Second, God is a responsive God, reacting to human needs and emergencies. He hears our prayers and takes action, although often not according to our expectations. God answered Hezekiah's prayer by healing him. God longs to hear from us through prayers that ask him to get involved with our lives and our problems.

When we don't invite God to get involved, the consequences can be severe. Take the case of King Asa (2 Chron. 14–16), a righteous king. Asa became afflicted with a serious disease in his legs. He did not seek God's help but instead *relied only on doctors*. He suffered in sickness for about three years and died. Unlike Hezekiah, Asa missed a cure because he didn't turn to the Lord in a time of trouble.

One man involves God in his crisis; the other does not. The two very different outcomes show how critical God's touch on our lives is. Faced with any health crisis, we must involve God through prayer.

PUTTING PRAYER TO WORK

A beautiful way to initiate that involvement is by reading the book of Psalms. Many of the psalms are prayers asking for physical healing, with praise for God's loving response. The psalms are useful as prayers because they put your thoughts into words—words that are honest expressions of your fears and desires. Examples of Psalms that can be used as prayers, as well as praise, include: 6, 23, 25, 30, 31, 103, 116, and 147. With each one, you'll be comforted by God's immovable presence.

LESSON OF THE DAY

Prayers are a part of God's healing process. He longs for us to ask for his intervention when we're sick. Involve him early and continually.

DAY 19

A Funny Thing Happened on the Way to Health

Automatically Reverse the Course of Other Bad Habits

With God's help, amazing things can happen after you kick your bad eating and no-exercise habits. Maybe you smoke, or drink too much alcohol. As you become physically more healthy and spiritually stronger, you'll be ready to give up other nasty habits as well. You'll feel naturally inclined to nurture your good habits and curb those that attract trouble.

Today, give serious thought to other poor health behaviors that may be blocking your path to total physical and spiritual fitness. You can use the principles covered thus far, along with professional help if necessary, to help you change other bad habits. For example:

- Remember that it's God's will for you to make healthy choices and live with regard for your health.
- Personalize the benefits of not drinking, quitting smoking, or kicking other bad habits.

- Take habit change one step at a time.
- Ask God to change you.
- Be prayerful about it.
- Look to Scripture.
- Enlist the support of family and friends.
- Physically remove temptations.
- Use spiritual resources to manage stress.
- Reward yourself for victories (See Day 20).

Take comfort, too, in knowing that changing your diet and becoming more active can have profound impact on other self-destructive habits. Research into addictive behaviors such as alcohol abuse and smoking reveals that adding nutrition and exercise to the treatment mix can aid in recovery. In a 1991 study reported in the *Journal of Substance Abuse Treatment*, 111 alcoholics entered a treatment program that included nutrition therapy and exercise. The program resulted in a recovery rate of 60 percent, considered very good. Other research on the relationship between physical activity and recovery shows that alcoholics who participate in a fitness program have higher abstinence rates after treatment than those who are not involved in such programs.

Studies show that involvement in endurance exercise can sometimes help cure a cigarette addiction. Exercise has also been used to help former smokers prevent relapses. In a study reported in the *Brown University Digest of Addiction Theory and Application*, researchers found that exercise prevented women who were former smokers from lighting up again for as long as a year after they had quit.

As you become physically strengthened by healthier choices, your desire for alcohol or cigarettes may diminish. Before long, old unhealthy behaviors will be replaced with new, healthy ones. Your life could take a whole new direction.

Years ago, I interviewed a Kentucky coal miner for a magazine article on wellness. He told me that once he had smoked three packs of cigarettes a day and could barely climb a flight of stairs. In danger of having a heart attack, he was warned by his doctor to stop smoking or go on a strict diet. Because he loved to eat, the miner decided to quit smoking. To his dismay, he gained twenty-five pounds. Then, a funny thing happened on his way to health.

Disgusted with his physical appearance, he decided to take up running. At first, he could barely run a quarter mile, and his neighbors laughed at him for trying. But he kept on, and after six months it got easier. He began to wonder what he could do, so he started running competitively, and eventually he became a marathon runner. You just never know where habit change may take you.

Moving forward to better health is a journey of great importance. You have the map and know the road signs along the way, but God is your Navigator. When you stop trying to struggle on your own and submit your will to God's, you'll find that his strength is sufficient to see you through. As you begin to let God act in your life, your tendency toward self-destructive habits will begin to fade away. You'll have a fresh start on life.

LESSON OF THE DAY

Like a line of dominoes, when one bad habit falls, down go all the rest, one by one.

Your Just Rewards

25 Ways to Celebrate Your Fitness Success

B ut as for you, be strong and do not give up, for your work will be rewarded" (2 Chron. 15:7). These encouraging words were spoken by the prophet Azariah to Asa, king of Judah, the ruler who early in his career had instituted many religious reforms. God promised to reward his work, and this spurred Asa on to a second phase of widespread religious reforms.

Rewards are great motivators; they have an activating and energizing effect on behavior. If promised an appealing reward, you have an extra inducement to perform. God uses rewards often in dealing with those who are faithful to him. His rewards have both earthly and heavenly significance. Living a Christ-centered life may bring rewards here on earth, but the best rewards await us in the life to come. The apostle Paul urges us to "run in such a way as to get the prize" (1 Cor. 9:24). Just as winning a race requires a strict diet and a rigorous training schedule, running toward our heavenly reward—in other words, making spiritual progress—takes the strict diet of God's Word and dedication to prayer, worship, and other disciplines of Christian living.

Throughout the Bible, rewards are promised to faithful believers who

- express personal faith in Christ
- follow Christ
- lead a righteous life
- lead a life of Christ-centered servanthood
- endure persecution for the cause of Christ
- remain devoted to prayer and worship
- share the gospel message
- disciple fellow believers
- delight in God's Word
- are kind to the poor and less fortunate
- love their enemies without expecting anything back
- give to the needy
- care for and love children
- extend hospitality to the righteous
- live a life of true humility.

Just as God does, we should regularly reward people who deserve it—at work, within our family, and even ourselves. Not only are rewards motivating, they're also encouraging, reinforcing, uplifting, nurturing, and transforming.

You're close to finishing the first twenty-one days of your new, healthier lifestyle. Perhaps along the way you've achieved an important marker—the addition of another mile or two to your walking program, some lost pounds, or some other important milestone achieved because you had the energy to push on. All the more reason to reward yourself.

Today, decide what your reward will be when you complete this 21-day program. But first, three rules:

1. Your reward should be a true treat—something you don't often do for yourself.
2. Choose rewards that make you feel physically attractive, emotionally uplifted, or spiritually inspired—or rewards that are just plain fun.
3. Your reward shouldn't tempt you to backslide. For instance, if you've just lost several pounds, don't reward yourself with a box of chocolate candy. Or if you've worked out faithfully for three weeks, don't treat yourself to a layoff from exercise.

Now the fun part . . . thinking up a reward for yourself. Here are some ideas:

25 FITTING REWARDS

1. Massage
2. New pair of exercise shoes
3. New sports gear or equipment
4. New exercise video
5. Weekend getaway
6. Camping trip
7. Shopping spree
8. New dress, suit, or other outfit
9. Makeover at a day spa
10. Facial
11. Pedicure or manicure
12. Salon haircut
13. Tickets to a concert
14. Jewelry
15. Healthy meal at a favorite restaurant (savored, not scarfed down)

16. Perfume or cologne
17. New CD or tape
18. Picnic
19. Limousine ride to a concert or other event
20. Flower arrangement, fresh or silk
21. Donation to your favorite charity (not all rewards need to be self-indulgent)
22. Basket of tropical fruit
23. New devotional, or other inspiring book
24. New addition to something you collect
25. Accessory or accent piece for your home.

LESSON OF THE DAY

Appropriate rewards give you the power to push on.

DAY 21

Well Done

How to Keep Feeling Vital and Healthy at All Times

Congratulations . . . you've done it!
Your God-guided choice-making has been transforming. Now it's time to feel good about what you've accomplished in only 21 days. Start by checking yourself out from head to toe. Look for body changes in the mirror. What do you see? A leaner profile? Taut, hard muscles? Better muscular definition? All of the above? Retrieve from your closet an item of clothing you always felt was a little snug. Try it on. If it's loose-fitting, you've lost some body fat. Throw it out to symbolize your newfound freedom from fat, or keep it around as a reminder of your former self. For some added reinforcement, look at an old photo of yourself. Hopefully, there's a noticeable difference since this "before" picture was taken.

But mirrors, clothes, and old pictures don't tell the whole story. You've got to look for changes elsewhere—for instance, in how you feel and perform. Do you have more energy?

Can you get more done in less time? By how much have you increased your activity in only three weeks' time?

Sometime soon, you might want to look into the "inner" you. Have a blood test to see if your cholesterol and triglycerides (a type of blood fat) levels have dropped as a result of your low-fat eating and active lifestyle. When those levels decline, your heart gets in better shape.

Emotionally, you may have it together a little better too. Perhaps you're less given over to emotional eating, or bouts of stress. Maybe your renewed prayer life has given you an inner peace that makes it possible to better handle whatever comes your way.

As you look over your body and your life, reflect upon your relationship with God. What has it been like to rely totally on him? Having a moment-to-moment relationship with God keeps you smack-dab in his will. When you're spiritually connected, nothing is impossible.

Today, list as many feel-great life-changes as you can, no matter how small they seem. Categorize them according to physical, emotional, and spiritual changes. Each day, you did at least one thing to make you feel better about yourself—so you should have a pretty long list.

Life-Changes So Far

Physical
A leaner, fitter body
Pants less tight around my waist
Healthier eating habits
More energy and greater stamina
Improved sleeping patterns
Improved general health

Emotional
Greater confidence
Less stress and anxiety
Better outlook on life

Spiritual

Better understanding of why God wants me to make healthier choices

More consistent prayer life

Success at dealing with unhealthy temptations

New attitude toward food

TURN BACK TO GO FORWARD

In just 21 days, with God's help and guidance, you've been physically, emotionally, and spiritually restored. The list you just made proves it. Naturally, you want to keep moving forward to crystallize your new healthy habits even more. But to forge ahead successfully, you've got to turn back. Sounds like a contradiction, doesn't it? But it's not. "Turning back" means going back to God and thanking him for all the changes you listed above. Some amazing things can happen if you do this.

On his way to Jerusalem, Jesus encountered ten men with leprosy (Luke 17:11–19). Because of their disease, the lepers stood at a distance from him, pleading to be healed. Jesus rewarded their faith by telling them to go and show themselves to the priests, who had the authority to pronounce them well. The men were obedient, and on the way to the priests, they were miraculously cured of their leprosy.

A curious thing happened next. One of the ten returned to Jesus, full of praise for God. The man fell on his face at the Lord's feet and thanked Jesus. Quick to point out that this man was the only one of the ten to turn back and give credit and thanks to God, Jesus said, "Rise and go; your faith has made you well" (v. 19). The word *well* can be translated *whole*. The thankful man was healed completely—physically and spiritually. Jesus saved his body from the incurable disease of leprosy and his soul from the incurable disease of sin. The latter was an extra blessing because the man had the gratitude to thank God.

Jesus responds to our turning back and giving thanks with additional blessings.

LESSON OF THE DAY

Celebrate your God-guided changes and thank him for the restoration that has taken place so far. God has extra blessings for the thankful.

EPILOGUE

Where Do I Go from Here?

*Cement the Foundation of a Happier,
Healthier Lifestyle*

I hope you found the last three weeks to be so effortless that you'll want to continue "living fit" ever after. To make your fitness victory a permanent one, here are additional strategies worth following:

• *Stay active.* The body, with its amazing system of muscles, joints, and bones, was meant to move. If the body doesn't move, its supporting structures like muscles and bones start degenerating. The exercising body is regenerating itself, especially with the right nutrients providing the raw material for growth, maintenance, and lifelong health and vitality.

• *Indulge yourself once in a while.* For 21 days you've been eating right consistently. Does that now mean "good-bye carrot sticks" and "hello chocolate cake"? Not exactly. You'll want to continue making healthy choices, day by day. But the good news is: It's healthy to indulge every now and then. Renouncing certain foods forever is a hard-to-keep vow—and trying to do so may only make you crave those foods more. Unless you loosen the reins occasionally, you could set yourself up for a pattern of overeating and bingeing. What's more, your long-term results won't be affected by an occasional nutritional infringement, especially if you're exercising regularly. You might try setting aside a day or two during the week (weekends are good) when you can indulge in some of your favorite foods, but without pigging out.

• *A slip is not a slide.* If you got a speeding ticket, you wouldn't quit driving. You'd pay the fine and try to obey the speed limit next time. Well, it's the same with healthy living. Don't let a setback make you throw in the towel. Forget the past and go back to square one. Resume your fitness program *one day at a time.* As you've discovered, even in a single day the rewards of feeling better start rolling in—and continue to each day, week, and month you stay true to a healthy lifestyle.

For some reassuring counsel on slips, read Psalm 94:18: "When I said, 'My foot is slipping,' your love, O LORD, supported me." If you ever find yourself slipping back into your old ways, God's love will sustain and strengthen you. Like a parent with outstretched arms to a toddler taking those first uneasy steps, God is there to pick us up, hold our hands, and steady our steps.

• *Maintain your reward system.* For every hour you exercise, put aside $5 or $10 toward a shopping account. Then use money from this account to buy yourself a reward whenever you need an extra nudge to stay with your program.

• *Expect success.* A study at the University of Pennsylvania surveyed the sales representatives of a large insurance company. Those who expected to do well sold 37 percent more than those with negative attitudes. The lesson here: Expect success and you'll achieve it.

Low expectations produce so-so results. It's both reasonable and realistic for you to expect to continue living a healthy lifestyle. After all, you've done it for 21 days—the time it takes to break bad habits and replace them with new ones. Confidence is built one success at a time, and you have 21 days of successes to keep you moving forward.

• *Get spiritually anchored.* There is a close connection between our spiritual and physical condition. Proverbs 3:7–8 says: "Do not be wise in your own eyes; fear the LORD and shun evil. This will bring health to your body and nourishment to your bones." Those who live a devout life, staying out of trouble and relying on God rather than on self, are potentially healthier and stronger because of their beneficial lifestyle. This advice is not a promise but a practical insight into the value of living as God intends us to live. Healthy choice-making is an act of obedience to God.

Eternally, though, there is only one choice that really matters. Not long ago, my husband, Jeff, and I updated our wills. Across the top of each will in large bold letters were the words "Last Will and Testament of . . ." At first glance those words relay the chilling shudder of finality. Until I realized, again, that both Jeff and I have already made life's most crucial choice: the choice to receive God's free gift of eternal life by accepting that Jesus paid for our sins on the cross, by asking him to forgive our sins, and by inviting him into our hearts as Lord and Savior.

I made this life-changing, soul-saving choice in the wake of a tragedy. After my mother got cancer and passed away, I began to think my own life through. What happens after death? Is there a heaven, and if so, how do I get there? God led me to a Bible-believing church, and in a few weeks I learned that there is indeed a heaven, where there is no sickness, evil, or death— but that you don't get in on the merit system.

Too many people assume that if they live a decent life, they can earn their way to heaven. They think that God has some divine scorecard by which he keeps track of how many good things you do. You know, like Santa Claus making a list and checking it twice. But what if someone else has a higher score than yours? Are you in or out? How many points do you need on your scorecard to be sure?

God makes it crystal clear in the Bible that there is only one thing to do. In John 3:36, Jesus plainly presents us with life's greatest choice: "Whoever believes in the Son has eternal life, but whoever rejects the Son will not see life, for God's wrath remains on him."

This is one of the most unequivocal passages in the Bible on how you can obtain eternal life. The operant word here is "believes." It does not mean a purely intellectual belief that Jesus is God; believing means placing your total trust and confidence in Jesus to take leadership in your life.

Jesus does not say, "Whoever tries to earn his way to heaven receives eternal life." Your eternal destiny hinges on one choice: to accept or reject Christ as your personal Savior. To reject Christ is a fatal decision. Why not be sure that the finish line of life is, for you, the starting gate of heaven?

At this very moment, Jesus is standing outside the door of your heart, softly knocking—not trying to bang the door down but beckoning to you: "Here I am! I stand at the door and knock. If anyone hears my voice and opens the door, I will come in" (Rev. 3:20). All you have to do is invite him to enter, live inside you in the person of his Holy Spirit, transform your life to conform to his . . . and one day, take you to heaven to be with him forever.

Where do you go from here?

APPENDIX

Fitness Foods

Eat-Right, Eat-Light Nutrition that Fills You Up Without Filling You Out

The U.S. Department of Agriculture has created excellent dietary guidelines for Americans, and these guidelines help ensure that you obtain maximum nutrition from your meals. Here's a look at how you can plan your meals according to the food groups established by the Department of Agriculture.

FOOD CHOICES AND SERVING SIZES

Bread, Cereal, Rice, and Pasta

Six to eleven servings. Your best choices in this group are the less-refined foods, such as whole grain cereals or brown rice. Eat more of the "pure" foods and less of the refined ones, such as breads or pastas. 1 serving = 1 slice of bread, 1 ounce of ready-to-eat cereal, 1/2 cup of cooked cereal, rice, or pasta.

Vegetables

Three to five servings. Vegetables are loaded with health-building nutrients. Try to eat a variety of vegetables in a variety of colors. Choose dark, leafy green vegetables, deep-yellow or orange vegetables, and starchy vegetables such as potatoes, sweet potatoes, and yams. 1 serving = 1 cup of raw leafy vegetables, 1/2 cup of other vegetables, cooked or chopped raw, 3/4 cup of vegetable juice.

Fruits

Two to three servings. Fruits are another food packed with health-building nutrients. Your best choices are fresh fruits and juices, and frozen or dried fruits. 1 serving = 1 medium apple, banana, orange, 1/2 cup of chopped, cooked, canned, or frozen fruit, 3/4 cup of fruit juice.

Milk, Yogurt, and Cheese

Two to three servings. Choose low-fat varieties to keep saturated fat in check. Saturated fat is found in animal foods and is responsible for elevating dangerous cholesterol in the body. 1 serving = 1 cup of skim milk, soy milk, or low-fat or nonfat yogurt, 2 ounces of processed low-fat or nonfat cheese, tofu, cottage cheese.

Meat, Poultry, Fish, Dry Beans, Eggs, and Nuts and Seeds

Two to three servings. Select low-fat varieties of animal proteins such as lean red meat, white meat poultry, and fish. 1 serving = 2–3 ounces of cooked lean meat, poultry, or fish, 1/2 cup of cooked dry beans, 1 egg, 2 egg whites, 2 tablespoons nuts or seeds.

Fats, Oils, and Sweets

Choose these foods sparingly.

Some foods fit into more than one group. Dry beans, peas, and lentils can be counted as servings in either the meat and beans group or the vegetable group.

When eating out, you can't measure portions accurately as you can at home. Plus, portion sizes at restaurants are getting bigger—in response to consumer demand. So chances are, you're eating more than you think and probably packing away more calories. To help you gauge what's on your plate, use the following measurement equivalents:

2 ounces of cheese = 1 domino.
1 serving of rice or cereal, or a potato = size of your fist.
1 serving of vegetables or fruit = tennis ball.
1 serving of meat, fish, or poultry = tape cassette, deck of cards, or your hand.

If you need to lose body fat, you may want to reduce your caloric intake, eat less fat, and control portion sizes. Here are some tips on easy ways to do this without sacrificing good nutrition:

- Eat a variety of foods that are low in calories and high in nutrients.
- Eat less fat and fewer high-fat foods.
- Eat smaller portions and limit second helpings of foods high in fat and calories.
- Eat more vegetables and fruits without fats and sugars added in preparation or at the table.
- Eat more whole grains and rice without fats and sugars added in preparation or at the table.
- Eat fewer sugars and fewer sweets (like candy, cookies, cakes, soda).
- Drink less or no alcohol.

Regular exercise is also important for losing body fat and maintaining a healthy weight.

Many people are not sure how much weight they should lose. Weight loss of only 5 to 10 percent of body weight may improve many of the problems associated with being overweight, such as high blood pressure and diabetes. If you are trying to lose weight, do so slowly and steadily. A generally safe rate is one-half to one pound a week until you reach your goal. Avoid crash weight-loss diets that severely restrict calories or the variety of foods.

REFERENCES

A portion of the information in this book comes from personal case studies, medical research reports in both the popular and scientific publications, professional textbooks, and computer searches of medical databases of research abstracts.

Preface

C. Everett Koop Foundation. *Shape Up America Report*, 1.

O'shea, M. "Better Fitness." *Parade* (December 18, 1994), 19.

U.S. Department of Health and Human Services. *Physical Activity and Health: A Report of the Surgeon General*. 1996. Atlanta: U.S. Department of Health and Human Services, Centers for Disease Control and Prevention, National Center for Chronic Disease Prevention and Health Promotion.

Day 1

Begley, S. "Beyond Vitamins." *Newsweek* (April 25, 1994), 44–49.

Brown, J. *The Science of Human Nutrition*. San Diego: Harcourt Brace Jovanovich, 1990.

Kleiner, S. M. "Antioxidant Answers." *The Physician and Sportsmedicine* 24 (1996): 21–22 .

Day 2

Allman, W. F. "The Mental Edge." *U.S. News & World Report* (August 3, 1992), 113–18.

Griffin, K. "Rebel Against a Sedentary Life." *Health* (April 1997), 82–88.

Lee, I. "Exercise and Physical Health: Cancer and Immune Function." *Research Quarterly for Exercise and Sport* 66 (1995): 286–91.

McBean, L. D., T. Forgac, and S. C. Finn. Osteoporosis: Visions for Care and Prevention—A Conference Report. *Journal of the American Dietetic Association* 94: 668–71.

Serraino, R. J. "Taking It All Off." *American Fitness* (March/April 1996), 43–44.

"The Health Benefits of Exercise: A Round Table." Part 1. *The Physician and Sportsmedicine* 15 (1987): 115–32.

"The Health Benefits of Exercise: A Round Table." Part 2. *The Physician and Sportsmedicine* 15 (1987): 121–31.

Day 3

Bloom, M. "Beat the Clock." *American Health* (June 1991), 44–45.

U.S. Department of Health and Human Services. *Physical Activity and Health: A Report of the Surgeon General*, 1996. Atlanta: U.S. Department of Health and Human Services, Centers for Disease Control and Prevention, National Center for Chronic Disease Prevention and Health Promotion.

Day 4

Wankel, L. M. "Personal and Situational Factors Affecting Exercise Involvement: The Importance of Enjoyment." *Research Quarterly for Exercise and Sport* 56 (1985): 275–82.

Day 6

C. Everett Koop Foundation. *Shape Up America Report*, 1.

Goodrick, K. G., and J. P. Foreyt. "Why Treatments for Obesity Don't Last." *Journal of the American Dietetic Association* 91 (1991): 1243–47.

Harris, C. E. "Dealing with a Relapse." *Shape* (September 1996), 196–202.

Day 7

Editor. "Seven Keys to the Good Life." *Tufts University Diet & Nutrition Letter* (August, 1, 1993).

LaForge, R. "Helping the Sandman." *Executive Health Report* (May 8, 1988).

Ludington, A. "Rest: How Much Is Enough?" *Vibrant Life* (March/April 1996), 4–6.

Nieman, D. C. "Oh, for a Good Night's Sleep." *Vibrant Life* (July/August 1995), 28–30.

Toufexis, A. "Drowsy America." *Time* (December 17, 1990), 78–84.

Day 8

Kashef, Z. "Your Partner in Health." *Essence* (November 1996), 32–34.

Morgan, D. V., and G. B. Bloch. "Mutual Motivation." *Health* (August 1988), 32–36.

Day 9

Fadiman, C., ed. *The Little, Brown Book of Anecdotes*. Boston: Little, Brown and Company, 1985.

Day 10

Zimbardo, P. "Social Processes. In *Psychology and Life*. 12th ed. Glenview, Illinois: Scott, Foresman and Company, 1988.

Day 11

Clark, N. "Fluid Facts: What, When, and How Much to Drink." *The Physician and Sportsmedicine* 20 (1992): 33–36.

_____. "What's Brewing with Caffeine?" *The Physician and Sportsmedicine* 22 (1994): 15–16.

Editor. "Hormones and Fatigue: What's the Connection?" *Menopause News*, (January/February 1996), 1–3.

Katz, N. "From Exhausted to Energized." *Mature Health* (February 1990), 36–39.

LaForge, R. "Enhancing Your Stamina at Home and Work." *Executive Health Report* (March 1990), 1–4.

Lark, S. "The Low-Energy Blues." *Vegetarian Times* (February 1992), 18–20.

McMurtry, J. J., and R. Sherwin. "History, Pharmacology, and Toxicology of Caffeine and Caffeine-Containing Beverages." *Clinical Nutrition* 6 (1987): 249–54.

Steadman, S. R. "Eight Ways to Get More Energy." *Natural Health* (September/October 1995), 66–68.

Day 12

C. Everett Koop Foundation. *Shape Up America Report*, 1

Editor. "Workouts Built for Two." *Weight Watchers Magazine* (February 1995), 38–41.

Horn, J. C. "The Best Way to Tough It Out." *Psychology Today* (November 1989), 72–74.

Martin, J. "Fitness Fun for the Whole Family." *American Health* (July/August 1995), 70–74.

Robison. J. I., M. A. Rogers, J. J. Carlson, B. E. Mavis, et al. "Effects of a Six-Month Incentive-Based Exercise Program on Adherence and Work Capacity." *Medicine and Science in Sports and Exercise* 24 (1992): 85–93.

Day 14

Dreher, H. "Hey, Lend a Helping Hand." *Natural Health* (January/February 1996), 54–56.

Fischman, J. "Type A on Trial." *Psychology Today* (February 1987), 42–48.

Geier, T. "Hotheads and Heart Attacks." *U.S. News & World Report* (November 11, 1996), 16.

Goleman, D. "Kicking the Doom and Gloom Worry Habit." *Cosmopolitan* (August 1989), 214–17.

Grady, D. "Think Right. Stay Well." *American Health* (November1992), 50–54.

Knaster, M. "The Good That Comes from Doing Good." *East West* (November/December 1991), 64–72.

Luks, A. "Helper's High: Volunteering Makes People Feel Good, Physically and Emotionally." *Psychology Today* (October 1988), 39–40.

Moran, V. "Mind Over Immunity." *Vegetarian Times* (November 1989), 32–36.

Day 15

Christofferson, T. "Those Out-of-Control Portions." *Vegetarian Times* (April 1997), 84–88.

Donaldson, K. A. "Medical/Nutrition Update." *Total Health* (June 1993), 8–9.

Editor. "Can I Get That with the Mayo on the Side?" *Forbes* (March 10, 1997), 90.

Day 18

Byrd, R. C. "Positive Therapeutic Effects of Intercessory Prayer in a Coronary Care Unit Population." *Southern Medical Journal* 81 (1988): 826–29.

Fadiman, C., ed. *The Little, Brown Book of Anecdotes.* Boston: Little, Brown and Company, 1985.

Day 19

Beasley, J. D. "Alcohol, Drug Addiction Recovery Rate Can Be Doubled with Program of Nutritional Support." *Health News & Review* (Summer 1995), 1–2 (originally reported in *The Journal of Substance Abuse Treatment* 8, [1991]).

"Exercise May Enhance the Maintenance of Smoking Cessation in Women." *The Brown University Digest of Addiction Theory and Application* (June 1995), 10.

Shepard, R. J. "Physical Activity, Health, and Well-Being at Different Life Stages." *Research Quarterly for Exercise and Sport* 66 (1995): 298–302.

Epilogue

Parachin, V. M. "Motivate to the Max." *Total Health* (December 1990), 30–32.

Appendix A

U.S. Department of Agriculture, U.S. Department of Health and Human Services. 1995. *Nutrition and Your Health: Dietary Guidelines for Americans.* 4th ed. Washington, D.C. (1995), GPO.

NOTES

DAY 9: Talk Yourself into Good Habits

1. From Glenn van Ekeren, *The Speaker's Sourcebook* (Englewood Cliffs, NJ: Prentice Hall, 1988). Used by permission.

DAY 17: Toward a New Food Attitude

1. In verse 4, God's exception was eating blood: "But you must not eat meat that has its lifeblood still in it." Pagans drank blood, believing it contained a lifeforce that would strengthen them. God wanted to discourage such pagan practices so that the Israelites would rely on his strength alone. From a health perspective, the prohibition against eating blood is a critical one, since many deadly diseases are transmitted by blood.

AUTHOR'S BIOGRAPHY

Maggie Greenwood-Robinson is one of the country's top health and medical authors. She is the coauthor of nine other fitness books, including the national best-seller *Lean Bodies, Lean Bodies Total Fitness, 50 Workout Secrets,* and *High Performance Nutrition.*

Her articles have appeared in *Let's Live, Shape Magazine, Women's Sports and Fitness, Working Woman, Muscle and Fitness, Female Bodybuilding and Fitness,* and many other publications. In addition, she has taught bodyshaping classes at the University of Southern Indiana. Maggie has a doctorate in nutritional counseling and is a certified nutritional counsultant.

Look for all eight books in the 21-Days Series

The **21-Day Series** is perfect for anyone wanting to affect positive changes in their life. Studies have shown that virtually any habit can be established in a 21-day period. That's the idea behind the **21-Day Series**. If you are willing to concentrate on one important habit, using a day-by-day plan for change, then you can make positive, lasting improvements in your life.

In **21 Days to Enjoying Your Bible**, youth leader and author Todd Temple shows you why the Bible is so fascinating, how to navigate its pages, how it is organized, and what personal, practical help the Bible offers. Softcover 0-310-21745-8

In **21 Days to Eating Better**, Gregory Jantz, who is founder and executive director of The Center for Counseling and Health Resources, uses proven strategies to teach you how to replace negative eating habits with energizing, healthy ways to feed and nurture not only the body but also your mind and soul. Softcover 0-310-21747-4

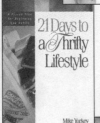

21 Days to a Thrifty Lifestyle by Mike Yorkey is all about spending money wisely, revealing practical ways to track expenses, how to save money, how to avoid being ripped off, and even includes plans for retirement, health care, and much more. Softcover 0-310-21752-0

21 Days to Better Family Entertainment by youth culture expert Bob DeMoss supplies sensible advice to help families regain control of TV, music, movies, the Internet, and other forms of home entertainment. Here's a creative, realistic approach to trading media overload for a better family life. Softcover 0-310-21746-6

In *21 Days to a Better Quiet Time with God*, author Timothy Jones shows readers how taking just a few minutes from their day to share with God can enrich their lives immensely. Softcover 0-310-21749-0

In *21 Days to Better Fitness*, leading health and fitness author Maggie Greenwood-Robinson offers readers a simple, day-by-day strategy for improving their fitness and health. Softcover 0-310-21750-4

21 Days to Helping Your Child Learn by Cheri Fuller is a short course in teaching kids the joys of thinking creatively and learning naturally. Softcover 0-310-21748-2

21 Days to Financial Freedom features a simple and practical financial plan that anyone can use, from the series' editor Dan Benson. Softcover 0-310-21751-2

ZondervanPublishingHouse
Grand Rapids, Michigan
http://www.zondervan.com

We want to hear from you. Please send your comments about this book to us in care of the address below. Thank you.

ZondervanPublishingHouse
Grand Rapids, Michigan 49530
http://www.zondervan.com